the overreachers

Books by Gay Talese

the over

reachers

by GAY TALESE

WITH ILLUSTRATIONS BY STANISLAV ZAGORSKI

HARPER & ROW, PUBLISHERS

NEW YORK, EVANSTON, AND LONDON

Most of the pieces in this book appeared first in *Esquire* magazine, to whose editor, Harold Hayes, I am deeply grateful. The rest of the material appears with permission and my thanks through the courtesy of the *Saturday Evening Post* (The Curtis Publishing Company) and The New York Times Company.—G.T.

FIRST EDITION

LIBRARY OF CONGRESS CATALOG CARD NUMBER: 64:20542

For **FLOYD PATTERSON**
an overreacher
who took that extra step

CONTENTS

OVER

You never have time to learn;
you are thrown in, are taught
the rules, and, the first time
they catch you off base, they
kill you.
  It is as Hemingway says.
  But the men who come later never
learn this. They make the same mistakes,
the same stupid, reckless, dramatic,
wonderful mistakes. They take that extra
step, climb too high, lean too far, go too fast,
get too grabby with the gods. They
seem to think that if they fleece
the gods, just once, they will become
immortal; it is an old Greek idea.
  They know, of course, that they will
die if caught, but they try anyway—and

REACHING

every once in a while one of them succeeds—
and experiences the ecstasy of cheating death,
and there is great rejoicing on earth, and
nobody asks if, perhaps, the gods threw
the game.
*   No man can think this way if he, too, craves*
the Great Moment; and so he also tries to do it
and top it, to go one step further, one peak
higher, to try things he should never try
because he is unequal to the task.
*   But he says, "Screw it." And sometimes he*
does, but more often he dies. Or sometimes
he neither does it nor dies—but,
*   Battered and torn,*
*   he half lives out the rest of his*
*   life remembering what a marvelous*
*   mistake it had been to try. . . .*

Young matadors were jealous of Mano-
lete and dared him, in 1947—when he
hoped to retire—to face the vicious
Miura bull he had long avoided.

So, before a bloodthirsty mob, he
tried to regain his mastery—and did,
until, hooked by a horn, he bled to
death.

They gave him two ears, a tail, and
a moment of silence.

Stirling Moss, whose gearbox had jammed, was two
laps behind with no chance to win when, strangely,
on a dangerous curve, he pushed to 105 m.p.h. and
tried to pass. He hit an embankment, broke half the
bones in his body.

Now he wonders: Why?

But his memory is gone. He might remember
through hypnosis, but then maybe all the old horror
will return.

Moss is very curious.

But not that curious.

In Chile, in 1925, on the night before he
would stunt-fly with the German ace Ernst
von Schonabeck, Jimmy Doolittle was walking on his hands along an officers' club window ledge that crumbled—dropped him
twenty feet, broke his ankles.

Next day, blind with pain, he insisted on
flying anyway; and, in a mock dogfight at
five thousand feet, it seemed his wheels were
scraping the German's wing.

When Doolittle landed, he denied this, saying he would never risk a man's life on such
foolishness.

Then the German landed.

His wings were ripped.

Other skiers in the 1939 Mount Washington (N.H.) Inferno raced down the 4,300-foot slope the sensible way, zigzagging, not exceeding 40 m.p.h.; but Toni Matt, deciding to ski in a straight line, soon was rocketing down at 60 m.p.h. . . . then 70 . . . then 80!

Then, losing control, he headed for a tree. But, as cheers chilled to silence, Matt lunged, missed it by inches, flew across the finish line a minute faster than the rest.

Nobody has tried it since.

Years later, Matt was discovered in Connecticut working quietly in a golf club as a greenkeeper.

George Leigh-Mallory was the man who, when asked, "Why Everest?" answered, "Because it is there."

Repeatedly he pursued its peak and, in 1924, with an oxygen expert from Oxford, he flawlessly ascended to 28,228 feet—just 800 from the top; and, from campsites below, a man could follow Mallory's tiny speck against the snow, in the mist, moving slowly toward a spot that promised God's view— and, when last seen, Mallory was still climbing.

Floyd Patterson

At the foot of a mountain in upstate New York, about sixty miles from Manhattan, there is an abandoned country clubhouse with a dusty dance floor, upturned barstools, and an untuned piano; and the only sounds heard around the place at night come from the big white house behind it—the clanging sounds of garbage cans being toppled by raccoons, skunks, and stray cats making their nocturnal raids down from the mountain.

The white house seems deserted, too; but occasionally, when the animals become too clamorous, a light will flash on, a window will open, and a Coke bottle will come flying through the darkness and smash against the cans. But mostly the animals are undisturbed until daybreak, when the rear door of the white house swings open and a broad-shouldered Negro appears in gray sweat clothes with a white towel around his neck.

He runs down the steps, quickly passes the garbage cans and proceeds at a trot down the dirt road beyond the country club toward the highway. Sometimes he stops along the road and throws a flurry of punches at imaginary foes, each jab punctuated by hard gasps of his breathing—"hegh-hegh-hegh-hegh"—and then, reaching the highway, he turns and soon disappears up the mountain.

At this time of morning farm trucks are on the road, and the drivers wave at the runner. And later in the morning other motorists see him, and a few stop suddenly at the curb and ask: "Say, aren't you Floyd Patterson?"

"No," says Floyd Patterson. "I'm his brother, Raymond."

The motorists move on, but recently a man on foot, a disheveled man who seemed to have spent the night outdoors, staggered behind the runner along the road and yelled, "Hey, Floyd Patterson!"

"No, I'm his brother, Raymond."

"Don't tell *me* you're not Floyd Patterson. I know what Floyd Patterson looks like."

"Okay," Patterson said, shrugging, "if you want me to be Floyd Patterson, I'll be Floyd Patterson."

"So let me have your autograph," said the man, handing him a rumpled piece of paper and a pencil.

He signed it—"Raymond Patterson."

One hour later Floyd Patterson was jogging his way back down the dirt path toward the white house, the towel over his head absorbing the sweat from his brow. He lives alone in a two-room apartment in the rear of the house, and has remained there in almost complete seclusion since getting knocked out a second time by Sonny Liston.

In the smaller room is a large bed he makes up himself, several record albums he rarely plays, a telephone that seldom rings. The larger room has a kitchen on one side and on the other, adjacent to a sofa, is a fireplace from which are hung boxing trunks and T-shirts to dry, and a photograph of him when he was the champion, and also a television set. The set is usually on except when Patterson is sleeping, or when he is sparring across the road inside the clubhouse (the ring is rigged over what was once the dance floor), or when, in a rare moment of painful honesty, he reveals to a visitor what it is like to be the loser.

"Oh, I would give up anything to just be able to work with Liston, to box with him somewhere where nobody would see us, and to see if I could get past three minutes with him," Patterson was saying, wiping his face with the towel, pacing slowly around the room near the sofa. "I *know* I can do better. . . . Oh, I'm not talking about a rematch. Who would pay a nickel for another Patterson-Liston match? I know *I* wouldn't. . . . But all I want to do is get past the first round."

Then he said, "You have no idea how it is in the first round. You're out there with all those people around you, and those cameras, and the whole world looking in, and all that movement, that excitement, and 'The Star-Spangled Banner,' and the whole nation hoping you'll win, including President Kennedy. And do you know what this all does? It blinds you, just blinds you. And then the bell rings, and you go at Liston and he's coming at you, and you're not even aware that there's a referee in the ring with you.

". . . Then you can't remember much of the rest, because you don't want to. . . . All you recall is, all of a sudden, you're getting up, and the referee is saying, 'You all right?' and you say, 'Of *course* I'm all right,' and he says, 'What's your name?' and you say, 'Patterson.'

"And then, suddenly, with all this screaming around you, you're down again, and know you have to get up, but you're extremely groggy, and the referee is pushing you back, and your trainer is in there with a towel, and people are all standing up, and your eyes focus directly at no one person—you're sort of floating.

"It's not a *bad* feeling when you're knocked out," he said.

"It's a *good* feeling, actually. It's not painful, just a sharp grogginess. You don't see angels or stars; you're on a pleasant cloud. After Liston hit me in Nevada, I felt, for about four or five seconds, that everybody in the arena was actually in the ring with me, circled around me like a family, and you feel warmth toward all the people in the arena after you're knocked out. You feel lovable to all the people. And you want to reach out and kiss everybody—men and women—and after the Liston fight somebody told me I actually blew a kiss to the crowd from the ring. I don't remember that. But I guess it's true because that's the way you feel during the four or five seconds after a knockout. . . .

"But then," Patterson went on, still pacing, "this good feeling leaves you. You realize where you are, and what you're doing there, and what has just happened to you. And what follows is a hurt, a confused hurt—not a physical hurt—it's a hurt combined with anger; it's a what-will-people-think hurt; it's an ashamed-of-my-own-ability hurt . . . and all you want then is a hatch door in the middle of the ring—a hatch door that will open and let you fall through and land in your dressing room instead of having to get out of the ring and face those people. The worst thing about losing is having to walk out of the ring and face those people. . . ."

Then Patterson walked over to the stove and put on the kettle for tea. He remained silent for a few moments. Through the walls could be heard the footsteps and voices of the sparring partners and the trainer, who live in the front of the house. Soon they would be in the country club getting things ready should Patterson wish to spar.

Patterson wants to continue as a prizefighter but his wife, whom he rarely sees any more, and most of his friends think he should quit. They point out that he does not need the money. Even he admits that from investments alone on his

$8,000,000 gross earnings he should have an annual income
of about $35,000 for the next twenty-five years. But Patter-
son, who is only twenty-eight years old and barely scratched,
cannot believe that he is finished. He cannot help but think
that it was something more than Liston that destroyed him—a
strange, psychological force was also involved—and unless he
can fully understand what it was, and learn to deal with it in
the boxing ring, he may never be able to live peacefully anywhere but under this mountain. Nor will he ever be able to
discard the false whiskers and mustache that, ever since
Johansson beat him in 1959, he has carried with him in a
small attaché case into each fight so he can slip out of the
stadium unrecognized should he lose.

"I often wonder what other fighters feel, and what goes
through their minds when they lose," Patterson said, placing
the cups of tea on the table. "I've wanted so much to talk to
another fighter about all this, to compare thoughts, to see if
he feels some of the same things I've felt. But who can you
talk to? Most fighters don't talk much anyway. And I can't
even look another fighter in the eye at a weigh-in, for some
reason.

"At the Liston weigh-in, the sportswriters noticed this,
and said it showed I was afraid. But that's not it. I can never
look *any* fighter in the eye because . . . well, because we're
going to fight, which isn't a nice thing, and because . . . well,
once I actually did look a fighter in the eye. It was a long,
long time ago. I must have been in the amateurs then. . . .
And when I looked at this fighter, I saw he had such a nice
face. . . . And then he looked at *me* . . . and *smiled* at me
. . . and *I* smiled back! . . . It was strange, very strange.
When a guy can look at another guy and smile like that, I
don't think they have any business fighting.

"I don't remember what happened in that fight, and I don't

remember what the guy's name was. I only remember that, ever since, I have never looked another fighter in the eye. . . ."

The telephone rang in the bedroom. Patterson got up to answer it. It was his wife, Sandra. So he excused himself, shutting the bedroom door behind him.

Sandra Patterson and their four children live in a $100,000 home in an upper-middle-class white neighborhood in Scarsdale, New York. Floyd Patterson feels uncomfortable in this home surrounded by a manicured lawn and stuffed with soft furniture, and, since losing his title to Liston, he has preferred living full time at his camp, which his children have come to know as "Daddy's house." The children, the eldest of whom is a six-year-old daughter named Jeannie, do not know exactly what their father does for a living. But Jeannie, who watched the last Liston-Patterson fight on closed-circuit television, accepted the explanation that her father performs in a kind of game where the men take turns pushing one another down; he had his turn pushing them down, and now it is their turn.

The bedroom door opened again, and Floyd Patterson, shaking his head, was very angry and nervous.

"I'm not going to work out today," he said. "I'm going to fly down to Scarsdale. Those boys are picking on Jeannie again. She's the only Negro in this school, and the older kids give her a rough time, and some of the older boys tease her and lift up her dress all the time. Yesterday she went home crying, and so today I'm going down there and plan to wait outside the school for those boys to come out, and . . ."

"How old are they?" he was asked.

"Teenagers," he said. "Old enough for a left hook."

Patterson telephoned his pilot friend, Ted Hanson, who stays at the camp and does public relations work for him, and has helped teach Patterson to fly. Five minutes later Hanson, a lean white man with a crewcut and glasses, was knocking on the door; and ten minutes later both were in the car that Patterson was driving almost recklessly over the narrow, winding country roads toward the airport, about six miles from the camp.

"Sandra is afraid I'll cause trouble; she's worried about what I'll do to those boys; she doesn't want trouble!" Patterson snapped, swerving around a hill and giving his car more gas. "She's just not firm enough! She's afraid. . . . She was afraid to tell me about that grocery man who's been making passes at her. It took her a long time before she told me about that dishwasher repairman who comes over and calls her *'baby.'* They all know I'm away so much. And that dishwasher repairman's been to my home about four, five times this month already. That machine breaks down every week. I guess he fixes it so it breaks down every week. Last time, I laid a trap. I waited forty-five minutes for him to come, but then he didn't show up. I was going to grab him and say, 'How would you like it if I called *your* wife *"baby"?* You'd feel like punching me in the nose, wouldn't you? Well, that's what I'm going to do—if you ever call her *"baby"* again. You call her Mrs. Patterson; or Sandra, if you know her. But you don't know her, so call her Mrs. Patterson.' . . . And then I told Sandra that these men, this type of white man, he just wants to have some fun with colored women. He'll never marry a colored woman, just wants to have some fun. . . ."

Now he was driving into the airport's parking lot. Directly ahead, roped to the grass air strip, was the single-engine, green Cessna that Patterson bought and learned to fly in Denver before the second Liston fight. Flying was a thing Patterson had always feared—a fear shared by, maybe inherited from, his manager, Cus D'Amato, who still will not fly.

D'Amato, who began training Patterson when the fighter was fourteen years old and exerted a tremendous influence over his psyche, is a strange but fascinating man of fifty-six who is addicted to spartanism and self-denial and is possessed by suspicion and fear: he avoids subways because he fears someone might push him onto the tracks; never has married because he believes a wife might be duped by his enemies; never reveals his home address because he suspects snipers.

"I must keep my enemies confused," D'Amato once explained. "When they are confused, then I can do a job for my fighters. What I do not want in life, however, is a sense of security; the moment a person knows security, his senses are dulled—and he begins to die. I also do not want many pleasures in life; I believe the more pleasures you get out of living, the more fear you have of dying."

Until a few years ago, D'Amato did most of Patterson's talking, and ran things like an Italian *padrone*. But later Patterson, the maturing son, rebelled against the Father Image. After losing to Sonny Liston the first time—a fight D'Amato had urged Patterson to resist—Patterson took flying lessons. And before the second Liston fight Patterson had conquered his fear of height, was master at the controls, was filled with renewed confidence—and knew, too, that even if he lost he at least possessed a vehicle that could get him out of town, fast.

But it didn't. After the flight, the little Cessna, weighed down by too much luggage, became overheated ninety miles outside of Las Vegas. Patterson and his pilot companion, having no choice but to turn back, radioed the airfield and arranged for the rental of a larger plane. When they landed, the Vegas air terminal was filled with people leaving town after the fight. Patterson hid in the shadows behind a hangar. His beard was packed in the trunk. But nobody saw him.

Later the pilot flew Patterson's Cessna back to New York alone. And Patterson flew in the larger, rented plane. He was accompanied on this flight by Ted Hanson, a friendly forty-two-year-old, thrice-divorced Californian, who once was a crop duster, a bartender, and a cabaret hoofer; later he became a pilot instructor in Las Vegas, and it was there that he met Patterson. The two became good friends. And, when Patterson asked Hanson to help fly the rented plane back to New York, Hanson did not hesitate, even though he had a slight hangover that night—partly due to being depressed by Liston's victory, partly to being slugged in a bar by a drunk after objecting to some unflattering things the drunk had said about the fight.

Once in the airplane, however, Ted Hanson became very alert. He had to be because, after the plane had cruised awhile at ten thousand feet, Floyd Patterson's mind seemed to wander back to the ring, and the plane would drift off course, and Hanson would say, "Floyd, Floyd, how's about getting back on course?" and then Patterson's head would snap up and his eyes would flash toward the dials. And everything would be all right for a while. But then he was back in the arena, reliving the fight, hardly believing that it had really happened. . . .

> ". . . And I kept thinking, as I flew out of Vegas that night, of all those months of training before the fight, all the roadwork, all the sparring, all the months away from Sandra . . . thinking of the time in camp when I wanted to stay up until 11:15

P.M. *to watch a certain movie on the Late Show, but I didn't because I had roadwork the next morning. . . .*

"And I was thinking about how good I'd felt before the fight, as I lay on the table in the dressing room. . . . I remember thinking, 'You're in excellent physical condition, you're in good mental condition—but are you vicious?' But you tell yourself, 'Viciousness is not important now, don't think about it now; a championship fight's at stake, and that's important enough and, who knows? maybe you'll get vicious once the bell rings.'

"And so you lay there trying to get a little sleep . . . but you're only in a twilight zone, half-asleep, and you're interrupted every once in a while by voices out in the hall, some guy's yelling, 'Hey, Jack,' or 'Hey, Al,' or, 'Hey, get those four-rounders into the ring.' And when you hear that you think, 'They're not ready for you yet.' So you lay there . . . and wonder, 'Where will I be tomorrow?' 'Where will I be three hours from now?' . . . Oh, you think all kinds of thoughts, some thoughts completely unrelated to the fight . . . you wonder whether you ever paid your mother-in-law back for all those stamps she bought a year ago . . . and you remember that time at 2 A.M. when Sandra tripped on the steps while bringing a bottle up to the baby . . . and then you get mad and ask: 'WHAT AM I THINKING ABOUT THESE THINGS FOR?' . . . and you try to sleep . . . but then the door opens and somebody says to somebody else, 'Hey, is somebody gonna go to Liston's

dressing room to watch 'em bandage up?'

"And so then you know it's about time to get ready. . . . You open your eyes. You get off the table. You glove up, you loosen up. Then Liston's trainer walks in. He looks at you, he smiles. He feels the bandages and later he says, 'Good luck, Floyd,' and you think, 'He didn't have to say that; he must be a nice guy.'

"And then you go out, and it's the long walk, always a long walk, and you think, 'What am I gonna be when I come back this way?' Then you climb into the ring. You notice Billy Eckstine at ringside leaning over to talk to somebody, and you see the reporters—some you like, some you don't like—and then it's 'The Star-Spangled Banner,' and the cameras are rolling, and the bell rings. . . .

"How could the same thing happen twice? How? That's all I kept thinking after the knockout. . . . Was I fooling these people all these years? . . . Was I ever the champion? . . . And then they lead you out of the ring . . . and up the aisle you go, past those people, and all you want is to get to your dressing room, fast . . . but the trouble was in Las Vegas they made a wrong turn along the aisle, and when we got to the end, there was no dressing room there . . . and we had to walk all the way back down the aisle, past the same people, and they must have been thinking, 'Patterson's not only knocked out, but he can't even find his dressing room.' . . .

"In the dressing room I had a headache. Liston didn't hurt me physically—a few days later I only

*felt a twitching nerve in my teeth—it was nothing
like some fights I've had: like that Dick Wagner
fight in '54 when he beat my body so bad I was
urinating blood for days. . . . After the Liston
fight, I just went into the bathroom, shut the door
behind me, and looked at myself in the mirror. I
just looked at myself, and asked, 'What happened?'
and then they started pounding on the door, and
saying, 'C'm'on out, Floyd, c'm'on out; the press
is here, Cus is here, c'm'on out, Floyd.' . . .*

*"And so I went out, and they asked questions,
but what can you say? . . . What you're thinking
about is all those months of training, all the con-
ditioning, all the depriving; and you think, 'I didn't
have to run that extra mile, didn't have to spar that
day,* I could have stayed up that night in camp and
watched the Late Show. . . . I could have fought
this fight tonight in no condition.' . . ."

"Floyd, Floyd," Hanson had said, "let's get back on
course. . . ."

Again Patterson would snap out of his reverie, and refocus
on the Omnirange, and get his flying under control. After
landing in New Mexico, and then in Ohio, Floyd Patterson
and Ted Hanson brought the little plane into the New York
air strip near the fight camp. The green Cessna that had been
flown back by the other pilot was already there, roped to the
grass at precisely the same spot it was on this day five months
later, on this day when Floyd Patterson was planning to fly it
toward perhaps another fight—a fight with some schoolboys
in Scarsdale who had been lifting up his six-year-old daughter's dress.

Patterson and Ted Hanson untied the plane, and Patterson got a rag and wiped from the windshield the splotches of insects. Then he walked around behind the plane, inspected the tail, checked under the fuselage, then peered down between the wing and the flaps to make sure all the screws were tight. He seemed suspicious of something. D'Amato would have been pleased.

"If a guy wants to get rid of you," Patterson explained, "all he has to do is remove these little screws here. Then, when you try to come in for a landing, the flaps fall off, and you crash."

Then Patterson got into the cockpit and started the engine. A few moments later, with Hanson beside him, Patterson was racing the little plane over the grassy field, then soaring over the weeds, then flying high above the gentle hills and trees. It was a nice take-off.

Since it was only a forty-minute flight to the Westchester airport, where Sanda Patterson would be waiting with a car, Floyd Patterson did all the flying. The trip was uneventful until, suddenly behind a cloud, he flew into heavy smoke that hovered above a forest fire. His visibility gone, he was forced to the instruments. And at this precise moment a fly that had been buzzing in the back of the cockpit flew up front and landed on the instrument panel in front of Patterson. He glared at the fly, watched it crawl slowly up the windshield, then shot a quick smash with his palm against the glass. He missed. The fly buzzed safely past Patterson's ear, bounced off the back of the cockpit, circled around.

"This smoke won't keep up," Hanson assured. "You can level off."

Patterson leveled off.

He flew easily for a few moments. Then the fly buzzed to

the front again, zigzagging before Patterson's face, then landed and proceeded to crawl across the panel. Patterson watched it, squinted. Then he slammed down at it with a quick right hand. Missed.

Ten minutes later, his nerves still on edge, Patterson began the descent. He picked up the radio microphone—"Westchester tower . . . Cessna 2729 uniform . . . three miles northwest . . . land in one-six on final. . . ." And then, after an easy landing, he climbed quickly out of the cockpit and strode toward his wife's station wagon outside the terminal.

But along the way a small man smoking a cigar turned toward Patterson, waved at him, and said, "Say, excuse me, but aren't you . . . aren't you . . . Sonny Liston?"

Patterson stopped. He glared at the man, bewildered. He wasn't sure whether it was a joke or an insult, and he really did not know what to do.

"Aren't you Sonny Liston?" the man repeated, quite serious.

"No," Patterson said, quickly passing by the man, "I'm his brother."

When he reached Mrs. Patterson's car, he asked, "How much time till school lets out?"

"About fifteen minutes," she said, starting up the engine. Then she said, "Oh, Floyd, I just should have told Sister, I shouldn't have . . ."

"*You* tell Sister; *I'll* tell the boys. . . ."

Mrs. Patterson drove as quickly as she could into Scarsdale, with Patterson shaking his head and telling Ted Hanson in the back, "Really can't understand these school kids. This is a religious school, and they want $20,000 for a glass window—and yet, some of them carry these racial prejudices, and it's mostly the Jews who are shoulder-to-shoulder with us, and . . ."

"Oh, Floyd," cried his wife, "Floyd, *I* have to get along here. *You're* not here, *you* don't live here, *I* . . ."

She arrived at the school just as the bell began to ring.

It was a modern building at the top of a hill, and on the lawn was the statue of a saint and, behind it, a large white cross.

"There's Jeannie," said Mrs. Patterson.

"Hurry, call her over here," Patterson said.

"Jeannie! Come over here, honey."

The little girl, wearing a blue school uniform and cap, and clasping books in front of her, came running down the path toward the station wagon.

"Jeannie," Floyd Patterson said, rolling down his window, "point out the boys who lifted your dress."

Jeannie turned and watched as several students came down the path; then she pointed to a tall, thin curly-haired boy walking with four other boys, all about twelve to fourteen years of age.

"Hey," Patterson called to him, "can I see you for a minute?"

All five boys came to the side of the car. They looked Patterson directly in the eye. They seemed not at all intimidated by him.

"You the one that's been lifting up my daughter's dress?" Patterson asked the boy who had been singled out.

"Nope," the boy said, casually.

"Nope?" Patterson said, caught off guard by the reply.

"Wasn't him, Mister," said another boy. "Probably was his little brother, Dennis."

Patterson looked at Jeannie. But she was speechless, uncertain. The five boys remained there, waiting for Patterson to do something.

"Well, er, where's Dennis?" Patterson asked.

"Hey, Dennis!" one of the boys yelled. "Dennis come over here."

Dennis walked toward them. He resembled his older brother; he had freckles on his small, upturned nose, had blue eyes, dark curly hair and, as he approached the station wagon, he seemed equally unintimidated by Patterson.

"You been lifting up my daughter's dress?"

"Nope," said Dennis.

"Nope!" Patterson repeated, frustrated.

"Nope, I wasn't lifting it," Dennis said. "I was just touching it a little . . ."

The other boys stood around the car looking down at Patterson, and other students crowded behind them, and nearby Patterson saw several white parents standing next to their parked cars; he became self-conscious, began to tap nervously with his fingers against the dashboard. He could not raise his voice without creating an unpleasant scene, yet could not retreat gracefully; so his voice went soft, and he said, finally, "Look, Dennis, I want you to stop it. I won't tell your mother—that might get you in trouble—but don't do it again, okay?"

"Okay."

The boys calmly turned and walked, in a group, up the street.

Sandra Patterson said nothing. Jeannie opened the door, sat in the front seat next to her father, and took out a small blue piece of paper that a nun had given her and handed it across to Mrs. Patterson. But Floyd Patterson snatched it. He read it. Then he paused, put the paper down, and quietly announced, dragging out the words, *"She didn't do her religion."*

Patterson now wanted to get out of Scarsdale. He wanted to return to camp.

After stopping at the Patterson home in Scarsdale and picking up Floyd Patterson, Jr., who is three, Mrs. Patterson drove them all back to the airport. Jeannie and Floyd, Jr., were seated in the back of the plane, and then Mrs. Patterson drove the station wagon alone up to camp, planning to return to Scarsdale that evening with the children.

It was 4 P.M. when Floyd Patterson got back to the camp, and the shadows were falling on the country club, and on the tennis court routed by weeds, and on the big white house in front of which not a single automobile was parked. All was deserted and quiet; it was a loser's camp.

The children ran to play inside the country club; Patterson walked slowly toward his apartment to dress for the workout.

"What could I do with those schoolboys?" he asked. "What can you do to kids of that age?"

It still seemed to bother him—the effrontery of the boys, the realization that he had somehow failed, the probability that, had those same boys heckled someone in Liston's family, the school yard would have been littered with limbs.

While Patterson and Liston both are products of the slum, and while both began as thieves, Patterson had been tamed in a special school with help from a gentle spinster; later he became a Catholic convert, and learned not to hate. Still later he bought a dictionary, adding to his vocabulary such words as "vicissitude" and "enigma." And when he regained his championship from Johansson, he became the great black hope of the Urban League.

He proved that it is not only possible to rise out of a Negro slum and succeed as a sportsman, but also to develop into an intelligent, sensitive, law-abiding citizen. In proving this, however, and in taking pride in it, Patterson seemed to lose part of himself. He lost part of his hunger, his anger—and as he walked up the steps into his apartment, he was saying, "I became the good guy. . . . After Liston won the title, I kept hoping that he would change into a good guy, too. That would have relieved me of the responsibility, and maybe I could have been more of the bad guy. But he didn't. . . . It's okay to be the good guy when you're winning. But when you're losing, it is no good being the good guy. . . ."

Patterson took off his shirt and trousers and, moving some books on the bureau to one side, put down his watch, his cufflinks and a clip of bills.

"Do you do much reading?" he was asked.

"No," he said. "In fact, you know I've never finished reading a book in my whole life? I don't know why. I just feel that no writer today has anything for me; I mean, none of them has felt any more deeply than I have, and I have nothing to learn from them. Although Baldwin to me seems different from the rest. What's Baldwin doing these days?"

"He's writing a play. Anthony Quinn is supposed to have a part in it."

"Quinn?" Patterson asked.

"Yes."

"Quinn doesn't like me."

"Why?"

"I read or heard it somewhere; Quinn had been quoted as saying that my fight was disgraceful against Liston, and Quinn said something to the effect that he could have done better. People often say that—*they* could have done better! Well, I think that if *they* had to fight, *they* couldn't even go through the experience of waiting for the fight to begin. They'd be up the whole night before, and would be drinking, or taking drugs. They'd probably get a heart attack. I'm sure that if I was in the ring with Anthony Quinn I could wear him out without even touching him. I would do nothing but pressure him, I'd stalk him, I'd stand close to him. I wouldn't touch him, but I'd wear him out and he'd collapse. But Anthony Quinn's an old man, isn't he?"

"In his forties."

"Well, anyway," Patterson said, "getting back to Baldwin, he seems like a wonderful guy. I've seen him on television and, before the Liston fight in Chicago, he came by my camp. You meet Baldwin on the street and you say, 'Who's this poor slob?'—he seems just like another guy; and this is the same impression *I* give people when they don't know me. But I think Baldwin and me, we have much in common, and someday I'd just like to sit somewhere for a long time and talk to him. . . ."

Patterson, his trunks and sweat pants on, bent over to tie his shoelaces, and then, from a bureau drawer, took out a T-shirt across which was printed *The Deauville*. He has several T-shirts bearing the same name. He takes good care of them. They are souvenirs from the high point of his life. They are from the Deauville Hotel in Miami Beach, which is where he trained for the third Ingemar Johansson match in March of 1961.

Never was Floyd Patterson more popular, more admired than during that winter. He had visited President Kennedy; he had been given a $25,000 jeweled crown by his manager; his greatness was conceded by sportswriters—and nobody had any idea that Patterson, secretly, was in possession of a false mustache and dark glasses that he intended to wear out of Miami Beach should he lose the third fight to Johansson.

It was after being knocked out by Johansson in their first fight that Patterson, deep in depression, hiding in humiliation for months in a remote Connecticut lodge, decided he could not face the public again if he lost. So he bought false whiskers and a mustache, and planned to wear them out of his dressing room after a defeat. He had also planned, in leaving his dressing room, to linger momentarily within the crowd and perhaps complain out loud about the fight. Then he would slip undiscovered through the night and into a waiting automobile.

Although there proved to be no need to bring the disguise into the second or third Johansson fights, or into a subsequent bout in Toronto against an obscure heavyweight named Tom McNeeley, Patterson brought it anyway; and, after the first Liston fight, he not only wore it during his forty-eight-hour automobile ride from Chicago to New York, but he also wore it while in an airliner bound for Spain.

"As I got onto this plane, you'd never have recognized me," he said. "I had on this beard, mustache, glasses, and hat —and I also limped, to make myself look older. I was alone. I didn't care what plane I boarded; I just looked up and saw this sign at the terminal reading 'Madrid,' and so I got on that flight after buying a ticket.

"When I got to Madrid I registered at a hotel under the name 'Aaron Watson.' I stayed in Madrid about four or five days. In the daytime I wandered around to the poorer sections of the city, limping, looking at the people, and the people stared back at me and must have thought I was crazy because I was moving so slow and looked the way I did. I ate food in my hotel room. Although once I went to a restaurant and ordered soup. I hate soup. But I thought it was what old people would order. So I ate it. And, after a week of this, I began to actually think I was somebody else. I began to believe it. . . . And it is nice, every once in a while, being somebody else. . . ."

Patterson would not elaborate on how he managed to register under a name that did not correspond to his passport; he merely explained, "With money, you can do anything."

Now, walking slowly around the room, his black silk robe over his sweat clothes, Patterson said, "You must wonder what makes a man do things like this. Well, I wonder too. And the answer is, I don't know . . . but I think that within me, within every human being, there is a certain weakness. It is a weakness that exposes itself more when you're alone. And I have figured out that part of the reason I do the things I do, and cannot seem to conquer that one word—*myself*—is because . . . is because . . . I am a coward. . . ."

He stopped. He stood very still in the middle of the room, thinking about what he had just said, probably wondering whether he should have said it.

"I am a coward," he then repeated, softly. "My fighting has little to do with that fact, too. I mean you can be a fighter— and a *winning* fighter—and still be a coward. I was probably a coward on the night I won the championship back from Ingemar. And I remember another night, long ago, back when I was in the amateurs, fighting this big, tremendous man named Julius Griffin. I was only 153 pounds. I was petrified. It was all I could do to cross the ring. And then he came at me, and moved close to me . . . and from then on I don't know anything, I have no idea what happened. Only thing I know is, I saw him on the floor. And later somebody said,

'Man, I never saw anything like it. You just jumped up in the air, and threw thirty different punches.' . . ."

"When did you first think you were a coward?" he was asked.

"It was after the first Ingemar fight."

"How does one see this cowardice you speak of?"

"You see it when a fighter loses. Ingemar, for instance, is not a coward. When he lost the third fight in Miami, he was at a party later at the Fontainebleau. Had I lost, 1 couldn't have gone to that party. And I don't see how he did. . . ."

"Have you no hate left?"

"I have hated only one fighter," Patterson said. "And that was Ingemar in the second fight. I had been hating him for a whole year before that—not because he beat me in the first fight, but because of what he did after. It was all that boasting in public, and his showing off his right-hand punch on television, his thundering right, his 'toonder and lightning.' And I'd be home watching him on television, and *hating* him. It is a miserable feeling, hate. When a man hates, he can't have any peace of mind. And for one solid year I hated him because, after he took everything away from me, deprived me of everything I was, he *rubbed it in*. On the night of the second fight, in the dressing room, I couldn't wait until I got into the ring. When he was a little late getting into the ring, I thought, "He's holding me up; he's trying to unsettle me— well, I'll get him!' "

"Why couldn't you hate Liston in the second match?"

Patterson thought for a moment, then said, "Look, if Sonny Liston walked into this room now and slapped me in the face, then you'd see a fight. You'd see the fight of your life because, then, a principle would be involved. I'd forget he was a human being. I'd forget I was a human being. And I'd fight accordingly."

"Could it be, Floyd, that you made a mistake in becoming a prizefighter?"

"What do you mean?"

"Well, you say you're a coward; you say you have little capacity for hate; and you seemed to lose your nerve against those schoolboys in Scarsdale this afternoon. Don't you think you might have been better suited for some other kind of work? Perhaps a social worker, or . . ."

"Are you asking why I continue to fight?"

"Yes."

"Well," he said, not irritated by the question, "first of all, I love boxing. Boxing has been good to me. And I might just as well ask you the question: 'Why do you write?' Or, 'Do you retire from writing every time you write a bad story?' . . . And as to whether I should have become a fighter in the first place, well, let's see how I can explain it. . . . Look, let's say you're a man who has been in an empty room for days and days without food . . . and then they take you out of that room and put you into another room where there's food hanging all over the place . . . and the first thing you reach for, you eat. When you're hungry, you're not choosy, and so I chose the thing that was closest to me. That was boxing. One day I just wandered into a gymnasium and boxed a boy. And I beat him. Then I boxed another boy. I beat him, too. Then I kept boxing. And winning. And I said, 'Here, finally, is something I can do!'

"Now I wasn't a sadist," he quickly added. "But I liked beating people because it was the only thing I could do. And whether boxing was a sport or not, I wanted to make it a sport because it was a thing I could succeed at. And what were the requirements? Sacrifice. That's all. To anybody who comes from Bedford-Stuyvesant in Brooklyn, sacrifice comes easy. And so I kept fighting, and one day I became heavyweight champion, and I got to know people like you. And you wonder how I can sacrifice, how I can deprive myself so much. You just don't realize where I've come from. You don't understand where I was when it began for me.

"In those days, when I was about eight years old, everything I got I stole. I stole to survive, and I did survive, but I seemed to hate myself. Even when I was younger, my mother told me I used to point to a photograph of myself hanging in the bedroom and would say, 'I don't like that boy!' One day my mother found three large X's scratched with a nail or something over that photograph of me. I don't remember doing it. But I do remember feeling like a parasite at home. I remember how awful I used to feel at night when my father, a longshoreman, would come home so tired that, as my mother fixed food for him, he would fall asleep at the table because he was that tired. I would always take his shoes off and clean his feet. That was my job. And I felt so bad because here I was, not going to school, doing nothing, just watching my father come home; and on Friday nights it was even worse. He would come home with his pay, and he'd put every nickel of it on the table so my mother could buy food for all the children. I never wanted to be around to see that. I'd run and hide. And then I decided to leave home and start stealing—and I did. And I would never come home unless I brought something that I had stolen. Once I remember I broke into a dress store and stole a whole mound of dresses, at 2 A.M., and here I was, this little kid, carrying all those dresses over the wall, thinking they were all the same size, my mother's size, and thinking the cops would never notice me walking down the street with all those dresses piled over my head. They did, of course. . . . I went to the Youth House. . . ."

Floyd Patterson's children, who had been playing outside all this time around the country club, now became restless and began to call him, and Jeannie started to pound on his door. So Patterson picked up his leather bag, which contained his gloves, his mouthpiece, and adhesive tape, and walked with the children across the path toward the club.

He flicked on the light switches behind the stage near the piano. Beams of amber streaked through the dimly-lit room and flashed onto the ring. Then he walked to one side of the room, outside the ring. He took off his robe, shuffled his feet in the rosin, skipped rope, and then began to shadowbox in front of a spit-stained mirror, throwing out quick combinations of lefts, rights, lefts, rights, each jab followed by a *"hegh-hegh-hegh-hegh."* Then, his gloves on, he moved to the punching bag in the far corner, and soon the room reverberated to his rhythmic beat against the bobbling bag—rat-tat-tat-*tetteta,* rat-tat-tat-*tetteta,* rat-tat-tat-*tetteta,* rat-tat-tat-*tetteta!*

The children, sitting on pink leather chairs, moved from the bar to the fringe of the ring, watched him in awe, sometimes flinching at the force of his pounding against the leather bag.

And this is how they would probably remember him years from now: a dark, solitary, glistening figure punching in the corner of a forlorn spot at the bottom of a mountain where people once came to have fun—until the country club became unfashionable, the paint began to peel, and Negroes were allowed in.

As Floyd Patterson continued to bang away with lefts and rights, his gloves a brown blur against the bag, his daughter slipped quietly off her chair and wandered past the ring into the other room. There, on the other side of the bar and beyond a dozen round tables, was the stage. She climbed onto the stage and stood behind a microphone, long dead, and cried out, imitating a ring announcer, "LADIEEEES AND GENTLE-MEN . . . tonight we present . . ."

She looked around, puzzled. Then, seeing that her little brother had followed her, she waved him up to the stage and began again: "LADIEES AND GENTLEMEN . . . tonight we present . . . FLOYDIE PATTERSON . . ."

Suddenly, the pounding against the bag in the other room stopped. There was silence for a moment. Then Jeannie, still behind the microphone and looking down at her brother, said, "Floydie, come up here!"

"No," he said.

"Oh, come up here!"

"NO," he cried.

Then Floyd Patterson's voice, from the other room, called: "Cut it out. . . . I'll take you for a walk in a minute."

He resumed punching—rat-tat-tat-*tetteta*—and they returned to his side. But Jeannie interrupted, asking, "Daddy, how come you sweating?"

"Water fell on me," he said, still pounding.

"Daddy," asked Floyd, Jr., "how come you spit water on the floor before?"

"To get it out of my mouth."

He was about to move over to the heavier punching bag—but just then the sound of Mrs. Patterson's station wagon could be heard moving up the road.

Soon she was in Patterson's apartment cleaning up a bit,

patting the pillows, washing the teacups that had been left in the sink. One hour later the family was having dinner together. They were together for two more hours; then, at 10 P.M., Mrs. Patterson washed and dried all the dishes, and put the garbage out in the can—where it would remain until the raccoons and skunks got to it.

And then, after helping the children with their coats and walking out to the station wagon and kissing her husband good-bye, Mrs. Patterson began the drive down the dirt road toward the highway. Patterson waved once, and stood for a moment watching the tail lights go, and then he turned and walked slowly back toward the house.

Joshua Logan

The theatre lights dimmed, and the jewels in the audience sparkled like a city seen at night from an airplane; then the music began, the curtain went up, and row upon row of bow-ties settled, like a flutter of black butterflies, into their seats.

It was the première performance of Mr. President *and, though the road reviews were disastrous and the show was un-improved at this Broadway opening, the audience rushed backstage at the final curtain with their furs and first-night faces to greet the director, Joshua Logan, with "Dah-ling, it was* mahvelous!" . . . *"Josh, congratulations!"* . . . *"Wonderful, Josh, wonderful!"*

He knew they did not mean it, and they *knew they did not mean it, but very little truth is exchanged backstage on open-ing nights; the newspaper critics panned the show, with one, John McClain of the* Journal-American, *asking: "Whatever became of the unerring hand of Mr. Logan?"*

The unerring hand, Mr. Logan would have liked to reply, had been tied behind his back by his associates during re-hearsals, but such a disclosure would be to no avail and hardly gracious; and so here he was, stung successively by three critical flops (the two others being *All American* and *There Was a Little Girl*)—knowing that his next Broadway play,

43

opening in six weeks, had better be good. Already there was talk around Sardi's that his directorial taste was lost in vulgarity, and some of his friends noticed with concern the increasing pressure he was subjecting himself to in *Tiger Tiger Burning Bright*. In 1941 and 1953, he had spent time in mental institutions.

From the very first week of *Tiger*'s rehearsals, at the Booth Theatre on Forty-fifth Street, there were tension, strange reactions, and uncertainty, and the actors—all but one of them Negroes—seemed suspicious of Logan and envious of each other's roles. Claudia McNeil, the star of *Tiger,* an enormous woman, very dark, glared silently each day at Logan, measuring him, seeming to possess in her attitude the secret of his weakness and the power to destroy him. And Joshua Logan, at fifty-four, white-haired, white-mustached, big and broad-shouldered but somehow soft and very pale, stood in front of this Negro cast of this play about a mother who dominates her children in a dream world she has created in Louisiana— a play that gradually, as rehearsals progressed, churned up more and more memories for Logan, haunting memories of his days in Mansfield, Louisiana, on his grandfather's cotton plantation, where, in his boyhood dreams, he often saw himself as a strong man riding through the streets of Mansfield standing on a horse, arms folded high across his chest. In real life, young Joshua Logan had recognized in himself not the slightest resemblance to his imaginary hero.

He saw himself as a flabby and effete boy who, after his father's early death, was reared on his maternal grandfather's plantation under the almost claustrophobic attention of females. There were his sister, Mary Lee, endlessly worrying about him; his Negro nurse, Amy Lane, often mad at him but always watching him through the kitchen window, and saying, "Mah, he walkin' jes like old Judge Logan!"; and there was his mother, Susan, who dressed him prettily, read him poetry, and tried to divert him from all that was crude or vulgar. One afternoon in the middle of a biblical movie, just before Judith of Bethulia sliced off the head of Holofernes, Susan Logan, not wanting Joshua to see it, blocked his view by pushing him under the seat; then she whispered, sharply, *"Think of fields of yellow daisies . . . think of fields of yellow daisies!"*

Susan Logan was an elegant, genteel lady of the Old South whose family, like that of her late first husband's (he was also named Joshua Lockwood Logan), had originally settled in South Carolina. The first Joshua Lockwood had come to America from County Kent, England, and died sixteen miles outside of Charleston in the middle 1700's. While carrying his remains for burial to Charleston, the cortège was attacked by a pack of wolves and was compelled to bury his bones by the roadside nine miles from Charleston, and the widow was so shocked that she quickly returned to England. But some years later one of her sons, also named Joshua Lockwood, returned to Charleston, and here his family later enjoyed a congeniality with two other Charleston families, the Logans and the Lees, and subsequently there was intermarriage; so today, Susan, descendant of the Lees, is not only the mother of the Broadway director—she is also his cousin.

By the 1830's some branches of the Lockwoods, Lees, and Logans had moved from South Carolina down into Alabama, and a generation later others moved into Northwest Louisiana, where Susan's father settled on a cotton plantation, into which she moved upon the death of her husband with her three-year-old son, Joshua, her infant daughter, Mary Lee, and that ruler of the rear of the house, Amy Lane.

Susan feared Mansfield; it was a largely uncultured pioneer town with little of the tradition of the Old South, the Charleston of her dreams, but tinged instead with the Wild West, with a certain accent on bad manners and maleness. Susan tried, as best she could, to see that none of the crudity of this town infected Joshua, and she succeeded even though one day, perhaps when a circus was moving into town, there suddenly registered in Joshua the image of the man riding through Mansfield standing up on a horse—a marvelous man, perfectly balanced; a free man, ignoring the reins.

As Joshua Lockwood Logan approached his teens, his grandfather began to complain that Susan was making the boy into a sissy. Joshua adored his grandfather ("I put Tabasco in my milk to please him"), and he soon became a superb swimmer, a subscriber to the Charles Atlas body-building course, and, at Culver Military Academy in Indiana—which Joshua attended because of his mother's remarriage in 1917 to Colonel Howard F. Noble, an administrator there—he also became trained as a light heavyweight boxer. Encouraged by Colonel Noble, to whom Joshua later dedicated his play *The Wisteria Trees,* he trained hard in the ring, eventually winning the boxing title of the platoon, the company, the battalion, and finally the regiment. But every time he won, and had his hand held high in victory, Joshua would moan to himself, "Oh, God!"—the triumph meaning he had to fight somebody else, and he hated it.

After Culver there was Princeton, a school selected by Joshua's mother because it was "nice" and "there would be less drinking there"; and after Princeton, where he became president of the Triangle Club, and after a trip to Moscow, where he studied for six months under Stanislavski, Joshua

Logan settled in New York and embarked on a career as a theatrical director. When Colonel Noble died, Joshua's mother drove up to New York and moved in with him; and later, when he was directing two shows at once—one in New Jersey by night, the other in New York by day—his mother would greet him at Pennsylvania Station each morning with a pint of fruit juice. "The way he finally got away from his mother," said a friend who knew him well, "was through the doors of an insane asylum—a door that locked."

After his first mental breakdown in 1941, from sheer exhaustion and dejection over his work, he recovered in a Philadelphia sanitarium and, by 1942, was back on Broadway directing a successful show, *By Jupiter.* In 1953, while rehearsing *Kind Sir,* and battling simultaneously with agents and lawyers over the film rights to Michener's novel *Sayonara,* Logan had another breakdown; a year later, he had recovered and had another hit, *Fanny.*

Now, nine years later, in these daily rehearsals of *Tiger Tiger Burning Bright,* adapted for the stage by Peter S. Feibleman from his novel *A Place Without Twilight,* Joshua Logan discovered that he was becoming so emotionally involved with the script, and identifying so strongly with its characters—and at the *same time* becoming intimidated by the actors, especially by Claudia McNeil, who he felt was acting like Amy Lane—that it seemed he might be involved once again with Mansfield, the source of his old wounds and boyhood complexities—and he knew, too, that he could ill afford the trip. He needed the success of this play, and he had many obligations, both mundane and financial: he and his wife, Nedda, had two children in private school; there was the upkeep on his fabulous apartment on the East River, and his directorial staff, and his film company, his chauffeur, his cook, his psychiatrist whom he visits five mornings a week, his big Connecticut home with its sprawling grounds and magnificently manicured gardens. Though Logan earns in the neighborhood of $500,000 a year, it somehow seems barely enough, and one evening after a hard day's rehearsal of *Tiger,* Logan left the theatre and said, wearily, "I work for gardeners and psychiatrists."

He went easy on the actors. When they fumbled their lines, he remained patient. He gave them the benefit of his knowledge of Southwestern diction—"down there they pronounce it *'LOU*-ziana,' not 'Lou-*EEZ*-iana,' "—and he would relieve the tension (or, at least, try) by telling anecdotes about past Broadway shows he had directed, about Mary Martin in *South Pacific,* and about *Mister Roberts,* all the while speaking with warmth, and admitting that he did not yet know all the answers about how to stage *Tiger,* and welcoming any actor's suggestions at any time. "I'm not a puppeteer," he would tell them, "I am simply an editor, a sort of audience, and a friend, an encourager that nobody should be scared of—or *angry* at."

Then, in the second week of rehearsals, things got worse. Parts of the first act were rewritten. The actors had to learn new lines and forget old ones. They were disgusted that the role of the male lead, the prowling son who is to symbolize the tiger cat, went to Alvin Ailey, a dancer. Even some of Logan's associates, who sat in the dark theatre each day watching, were becoming uneasy.

"Goddamnit, Josh, that Alvin just doesn't move like a tiger!"

"No," Logan admitted, "he's Nijinsky."

"For that part you need a black Brando."

"Yes," said Logan.

"We open in three weeks."

"Christ!" said Feibleman.

"Oh, don't worry," said Oliver Smith, the co-producer.

"I *am* worried," said Logan.

The next day, after Ailey had played a sultry scene with the curvaceous, hip-swinging Diana Sands, he suddenly flew across the stage and buried his face in a corner behind the curtain. There was silence for a second. Then, slowly, the theater began to echo with what sounded like high, howling laughter; then, more quickly, the laughter dissolved into uncontrollable, almost hysterical sobbings. Everybody was stunned; nobody moved—either on the stage or in the orchestra.

Finally, Peter Feibleman, who had been sitting near the back of the theatre, came rushing down the aisle to Logan, sitting in the seventh row.

"Josh," Feibleman whispered, very upset, "you better do something."

"What can *I* do?" Logan said, running his hand through his long white hair. "He'll just have to get it out of him."

"I want the Miltown concession on this play," said Joe Curtis, one of Logan's assistants, sitting across the aisle.

"Trouble is," Logan said, "I'll take it all." Then, shaking his head as Ailey's sobbing continued, with Claudia McNeil now comforting him, Logan said to Curtis, "You know, I'm getting a real vicarious pleasure out of this. Alvin's doing just what I want to do—just lie down and cry!"

Still, Logan, Feibleman, and Oliver Smith all thought Ailey could do the part; he certainly *looked* the part, they agreed, possessing a muscular body and the arms of a weight lifter; and besides, it was a little late to be shopping around for a new tiger. Logan felt that, if the book was stronger, the actors would feel more secure; so for the next three days Logan disappeared with Feibleman in a little room offstage and reworked the book—urging Feibleman to remove some of the literary flavor in spots where Logan felt the audience would want action.

"Where the hell *is* Logan?" Claudia McNeil grumbled, on the third morning of rehearsing lines under the production stage manager, David Gray. Claudia was still smoldering at Logan for having left the theatre at midafternoon earlier in the week without having "the courtesy, the respect" to let her know he'd not return that day; now, with Logan working elsewhere on the script and ignoring the acting completely, Claudia was preparing to get even. With the other actors gathered around her offstage, as in a family scene in the play itself, she roared: "Logan should be here! We ain't gettin' no direction!"

"And our reputations are at stake," Diana Sands said.

"His is, too!" Claudia snapped. "He don't realize it, but if he thinks he gonna blame this one on me if it's a flop, well, he ain't; I jes get on that phone and call Sally Hammond over at the *Post,* or that guy at the *Tribune*—whatshisname? one that married that actress? Morganstern, that's it—and I'll tell 'em the whole story, about how we gotta come here and listen to nine of his jokes, and all about *LOU*-ziana and then he don't show up for three days!"

The others nodded, and she went on, "All this rewriting should be done at night! What the hell does he do at night? *Sheet!* People gonna look at me and think I shot my bolt in *Raisin in the Sun* and I ain't got nuthin new to offer; well, that ain't fair. . . . I got enough trouble, working with a lot of kids in this show, and carrying the responsibility for my whole race, being in the theatre thirty years, and this man Logan don't even show up! *Sheet!*"

A few minutes later, the door swung open, and in walked
Logan, followed by Peter Feibleman, who was carrying fresh,
revised pages of Act I. As Logan waved and walked down the
side steps off the stage toward the orchestra, Claudia watched
him go up the aisle toward the back of the theatre, and she
waited; within ten minutes, she saw her chance.

In the middle of one of her monologues, Claudia caught a
glimpse of Logan whispering to Feibleman. It was as if she
were Amy Lane catching Joshua's little hand in the cookie
jar. Flaring up, Claudia bellowed to Oliver Smith, the co-
producer, sitting alone about nine rows back, *"Mr. Logan is
talking! And I can't go on!"*

"I am *not* talking," Logan yelled from the back, his voice
tense and angry.

"You *were* talking," Claudia said. "I could hear what you
were saying!"

"I was *not* talking," he insisted. "Somebody else was talking. It was *not* me!"

"You were talking!" she shouted, hunching her big shoulders and blazing her big eyes at him. "And you spoiled the
meter of my speech!"

"Look," Logan said, stomping down the aisle toward
where Oliver Smith sat, "I do not want any more rages from
you!"

"You're in a rage, not me!" she said.

"Well, I'm not going to stand for this!"

"You want me to leave?" she asked, challengingly.

"Look," he said, more softly, "everybody here is trying
to get this play. I cannot *stand* these outrages. What do you
want us to do, close the show?"

Claudia now turned, hunched her shoulders again, and
shuffled around a bit.

"Now," Logan said, trying to get things moving again,

noticing that the cast was standing in almost fixed, dumb-struck poses on the stage. "Now, why don't you go back further and begin again?"

"I *can't* begin," she said, casually. "You spoiled my meter."

"Oh-h-h-h, Oliver," Logan groaned, his hand on his fore-head, "I can't stand these rages!"

"Well," she shot in, "that's *your* problem."

"You're my problem!" Logan screamed.

Now everybody in the theatre was squirming. Fortunately, Claudia did not answer him; she just shuffled around a bit, like a sumo wrestler waiting for the decision; in the pro-longed silence, things calmed a bit, and Claudia did her monologue and David Gray yelled, "Curtain," and every-body sighed. There was a break.

Standing outside the Booth Theatre, his hands in his pockets and the cold breezes of winter whistling through his long, thinning white hair, Joshua Logan said, "Right now I'm allowing Claudia McNeil to do a lot of things just be-cause I trust her, and admire her creative talent, and do not want to freeze that talent, and yet I know I have a block with her.

"You see," he said, "Amy Lane, every once in a while, would get mad and her face would turn gray. When Amy Lane was happy her face was brown, sometimes purple; but she used to scare me when she was mad; and when she was happy she used to help me, dress me, tie up my shoelaces and do my buttonholes; and now I've got this show and a sort of Amy Lane that every once in while turns gray. And I want to help her—I've *got* to help her—figure out the creative shoelaces and buttonholes. And sometimes I wonder if I'm strong enough to do that."

He walked around a bit more, inhaling deeply along Shubert Alley next to the theatre. "It's funny," he finally said, "but somehow I'm actually happy doing this play. Maybe it's the Negroes. Somehow, in a small way, I'm making up for . . . for how they have been made to feel. I don't know. But *something* must be making me happy. I remember, as a child, wanting to *be* a Negro; I remember their sweetness, their gentle voices, and mostly their freedom—they were free to run and run without shoes, without clothes; they didn't have to be clean, didn't have to go to church three times a week. They did not have, in the modern term, to conform. In a sense," he said, slowly, "they ruled *us*—kind of kept us in our place; they were more powerful, the power of the weak; only they weren't weak, they had the power of servilitude."

Now he was back in the dark theatre, the lights of the stage beaming on the actors going through a scene in the garden of their Louisiana shack; Claudia McNeil's voice was now softer because she had had a touch of laryngitis a few days before. But, at the end of the scene, she raised her voice to its full power, and Logan, in a pleasant tone, said, "Don't strain your voice, Claudia."

She did not respond, only whispered to another actor on stage.

"Don't raise your voice, Claudia," Logan repeated.

She again ignored him.

"Claudia!" Logan yelled. "Don't you give me that actor's vengeance, Claudia!"

"Yes, Mr. Logan," she said, with a soft, sarcastic edge.

"I've had enough of this today, Claudia."

"Yes, Mr. Logan."

"And stop Yes-Mr.-Logan-ing-me."

"Yes, Mr. Logan."

"You're a shockingly rude woman!"

"Yes, Mr. Logan."

"You're being a beast."

"Yes, Mr. Logan."

"Yes, Miss Beast."

"Yes, Mr. Logan."

"Yes, Miss Beast!"

Suddenly, Claudia stopped. It dawned on her that he was calling her a beast; and now her face was gray and her eyes were cold, and her voice almost solemn as she said: "You . . . called . . . me . . . out . . . of . . . my . . . name!"

"Oh, God!" Logan said, smacking his forehead with his hand.

"You . . . called . . . me . . . out . . . of . . . my . . . name."

She stood there, rocklike, big and angry, waiting for him to do something.

"Oliver!" Logan said, turning toward the co-producer, who had lowered his wiry, long body into his chair as if he were in a foxhole. He did not want to be cornered into saying something that might offend Logan, his old friend, but neither did he want Claudia McNeil to come barreling down the aisle and possibly snap his thin frame in half.

"Oliver," Logan went on, "I just don't know what to do with her. She's like some empress up there, or something. . . ."

"You're the empress!" she bolted back.

"All right, all right, I'm the empress," Logan said, too weary to argue about it. "What do we do now?"

"Get yourself another actress," she said.

"All right, fine," Logan said. "Fine," he repeated, "we can close the show, and, we can . . ." Now he was walking up the aisle, and it seemed that he might be leaving the theatre.

"Look," Claudia quickly said. He stopped.

"Look," she began again, as it dawned on her that if this show closed *she* would be the reason for all the other actors' unemployment, "I . . . I gotta man at home I can get mad at . . . and I been in the theatre thirty years . . . and nobody ever gonna point a finger at me that I walked offa show . . . and . . ."

She went on like this, and Logan knew he had her; he could have played with her awhile, letting her sweat it out, but he didn't. Instead he walked toward the stage, climbed it, and then, faster now, he moved toward Claudia and, arms outstretched, moved in to her, his white mustache pressing against her cheek—and then, dramatically, her big, black arms lashed around the back of his white shirt and pulled him close.

They were almost tearful in their reunion, these two big, soft figures under the lights; they suddenly were spent, and the cast gathered around and whistled, hollered, and clapped.

Then, cheerfully, Claudia pushed Logan again and, grinning as she shook her fist, said, "But when this show is over, I'm gonna hit you in the mouth *so-o-o* hard!"

"When this show is over," he laughed back, "you won't be able to catch me!"

"I'll catch you," she promised.

"You'll need a long reach," he said, "because I'll be *gone!*"

After this scene, the show improved tremendously in the final two weeks. Nobody was saying it was going to be a hit; but they *were* saying it would at least open. Claudia was not sure if Logan would condone another shooting match, so she calmed down. Logan, of course, did not look for trouble. If, while Claudia was rehearsing on stage, he wished to get some fresh air, he did not leave by way of the stage door (where she might see him) but would often slip through the darkness near the back of the theatre—an operation that meant he had to unhinge four latches and a lock and move quietly, much as he might have sneaked out of the house in Mansfield hoping Amy Lane would not hear. Then, on returning, he would be just as quiet; Claudia would be on stage but would not hear him: he was safe.

In addition to the improved relations between Logan and Claudia, the script was much better and Alvin Ailey had mastered the difficult tiger role, partly through Logan's help and partly because he got control of himself. Al Freeman, Jr.'s, portrayal of Ailey's weak brother produced some fine comic acting, and the play was also strengthened by two late additions—Roscoe Lee Browne, who played the sinister clergyman who blackmails Ailey, and Paul Barry, the only white actor in the show, who won the part as a seedy Louisiana redneck over five other actors, one of them an old acquaintance of Joshua Logan's from *Mister Roberts*. Logan greeted his *Mister Roberts* friend warmly, but soon realized that the actor was portraying the redneck as if he were a naval officer, and so Logan shook his hand—"Thanks, Bob, but I think, chemically, and from the point of view of age, you're not right for the part"—and then Logan said to Feibleman, "You can't go back, can you, Peter?"

"You sure can't, Josh," Feibleman said, quietly.

But if Logan were able to go back, there is no doubt it would be to the days of *Mister Roberts,* which he described as those "high, happy times," with that tragic young novelist Thomas Heggen. They got along famously as co-authors of the play, Logan said, because "I was a corpulent manic depressive and Heggen was a thin manic depressive." Sprawled out one night on a red, yellow, and blue rug that Nedda had bought at a Bridgeport junk shop, Logan and Heggen dashed off the whole second act in one hilarious session. The show ran on Broadway for 1,157 performances.

These were the days when Howard Lindsay declared that Logan was a "genius" and the late Oscar Hammerstein II said Logan was blessed with everything a great director should have—a good eye for pictorial composition and movement, an ear for dialogue and diction, a charm that keeps a big company working happily together, a talent for analyzing a script and improving it by criticism and revision. Playwright Paul Osborn then said that Logan could not "walk along a street and watch a kid pick a cigarette butt up out of the gutter without wanting to grab the kid and tell him how to pick it up better."

Then, in May, 1949, Heggen, who was unable to get his own writing going again, drowned in his bathtub. He was twenty-nine years old. But Logan has tried to hold on to the memory of the glorious days of *Mister Roberts;* he has named his son Thomas Heggen Logan, and still keeps the old red, yellow, and blue rug from the junk shop in an honored place in his Connecticut home.

Logan has had many triumphs since then—*South Pacific, The Wisteria Trees, Picnic*—but he still looks back on *Mister Roberts* as the high point, and still says, slowly and rather sadly, "That was the happiest time of my life."

In 1953 Logan was back in Louisiana to open *Kind Sir* in New Orleans, and was battling at the same time to get the screen rights to *Sayonara,* and then, almost too suddenly to know how it all happened, he found himself one day back in Mansfield. He wandered about the old plantation. He looked at the wisteria tree that his grandfather had been unable to chop down. Then, not quite realizing what he was doing, Joshua Logan crawled back into Jolly Den, the playhouse that his grandfather had built long ago for Joshua and Mary Lee. Then Logan drove back to New Orleans. He committed himself to De Paul Hospital.

"You ask if I shall finally be able to stop going to the psychiatrist," he said, walking across Third Avenue toward his apartment one evening a week before the opening of *Tiger Tiger Burning Bright*. "Well, I don't really know. You ask what's the matter with me, what it is that keeps me from being satisfied or completely happy, or smug, or completely serene about my life, and I think it is something that happened to me when I was a young boy and set a standard for myself that I could never live up to. I could never be as good as I wanted to be—would never ride through Mansfield standing on a horse with my arms folded high in front of me."

This does not mean that Logan has failed to make *some* peace with himself in his later years; for one thing, he said, almost proudly, "I have finally stopped being a shit kicker. Know what a shit kicker is, don't you? That's one of those modest bastards, those falsely modest, aw-shucks guys"— and he demonstrated by walking, hands in pockets, head down, with feet dragging. No, he is by no means modest, he said, even though his mother is a bit disappointed in him, and once, after he had reminded her that he was a Pulitzer Prize winner (for writing the stage version of *South Pacific*), she reminded him that *that* was for a collaboration—letting him know she knew the difference between a man who could win such a prize and a man who could ride the horse *alone*.

"Anyway," Logan went on, "I know what I can do. I know I have the ability to organize accident. I know I can pump people full of confidence. I can reassure a person who is in doubt. I know that every artist is in despair, and to allow them more despair would kill hope, and so I try to bring hope and banish despair. When I feel it coming on, I will it away, when I can—I not always can—but I know if I should panic in the midst of a big production then the production would fall apart. I have directed people who, they say, couldn't be directed, such as Marilyn Monroe, and I knew she needed affection, respect, love, and care, and so that's what I gave her, and no matter how her panic showed, I never let it make me angry or impatient.

"But," he continued, now more slowly, thinking more deeply, "I think if I were free of whatever it is—if I were free-*er*—I think I could write . . . and write more than Marcel Proust . . . couldn't *stop* writing. But it is as though it were all dammed up to here," he said, gripping his throat with his left hand, "and I have a theory—*just* a theory—that, if I wrote, it would please my mother *too much*. It would be too much what my mother wanted. And maybe . . . maybe *then* I'd become like my father. And I would die."

Now Logan was silent the rest of the way home. Then, on the fourteenth floor, the locale of his grand apartment overlooking the East River, he was greeted at the door by the butler and, in the next room, by Nedda, an erect, smiling, lovely woman who was his leading lady in one of his first big Broadway hits, *Charley's Aunt,* and who has remained constant through all his good and bad days. While Logan went into the other room for a moment, Nedda talked about their seventeen years of marriage that began, on December 8, 1945, with a civil ceremony in Greenwich, Connecticut; then they drove back to New York to inform Susan, who said, according to Nedda, "Well, isn't that lovely. Let us have a little glass of sherry."

When Joshua returned to the room, and realized the conversation had gotten back to his mother, he joined Nedda in telling their favorite Susan Noble stories. Joshua recalled that once he received a letter from her telling him that one of his relatives had just been drafted, and was being sent to Fort Bragg, North Carolina, and how nice it was for the drafted relation to be in North Carolina "at rhododendron time."

And Nedda recalled a family trip they all made a few years ago to Charleston, during which a visit was made to the cemeteries where the earlier Lockwoods, Lees, and Logans were buried. Upon seeing these familiar names on the gravestones, these names she had so long worshiped, Susan suddenly was as graceful as a young ballerina, picking her way delicately and joyously and whirling around; finally, seeing Nedda with a camera, Susan pulled Josh toward her and asked Nedda to shoot a picture of the two of them standing next to the tomb of a very special ancestor. "Stand *here*, Josh . . . over *here*," Susan snapped, because Josh was too far from the gravestone, *"here,* next to Dorothea . . . *she's* the important one; she's the one that makes us cousins!"

They told other stories about Susan, too, and 'Josh concluded, "Oh, she'll fascinate you!"

"She's seventy-six," said Nedda, "and she'll outlive us all."

"You *should* meet her," Logan said.

A few days later, on one of New York's most unseasonably warm wintry days, Susan Noble opened the door of her apartment. Behind her, under the mantel, a big fire was blazing. "Good morning," she said, smiling. "I hope you don't mind the fa'ar."

She was a remarkable-looking woman, not seeming much older than fifty, with gray-blue eyes, a trim figure, and hair that was still black streaked with gray, and pulled back from her face, which was soft, gentle, and vivacious. In the vestibule hung a portrait of Colonel Noble, straight-spined in military splendor; on another wall, a print by William Blake; and, in the living room, there was furniture from the South—from the plantation, some of it in the family for several generations. After pouring coffee and serving cookies, she displayed, on request, that which she treasures, the family album, and in no time at all her alert eyes were sparkling, her hand was moving softly over the pages, and her voice was dramatically rich.

"Look," she said, smiling at the little figure of Joshua in a colonial outfit, "pink satin. See! I did the coat. . . . And *here* is little May-rey. . . . And this was my mother's voice teacher. Wasn't she pretty? . . . And this, now *this* was my great aunt. . . . And look at that dapper! Oh, I just adore that man, one of my cousins, Henry Lee! . . . And now this, this is Grandfather Lee, John Bachman Lee, named after old Dr. John Bachman, you know, a friend of Audubon, with many birds named Bachman. . . . And this, sitting next to John McHenry Nabors, is Nimrod, the dog named for that great hunter in the Bible. . . ." And then, at the mention of her father, she paused. "He thought I was pulling Josh too hard, but little Josh grew up loving beauty. My father felt I was making Josh into a sissy, but that was not true. He was a man—a man from the time he was a child. And I did all I could to make him a man. That's all I *could* do! I couldn't play baseball. But," she said, "I also felt that a man has a right to that which is beautiful in life."

Then she glanced down at the book again. "Look," she said, her eyes once more sparkling, "here's Caroline Dorothy

Logan, Josh's great-great-grandmother. . . . And here, here's Josh again! . . . And here, I believe, is Nedda. . . ."

On Saturday night, a few days later, outside the Booth Theatre, all dressed up—as in a picture album—they came to see *Tiger Tiger Burning Bright*. There was Susan Noble arriving early . . . and next Nedda, in a fur cape and red satin dress . . . and Logan's assistant, Joe Curtis . . . and Oliver Smith . . . and Peter Feibleman, a white carnation in his trimly-tailored tuxedo . . . and there were Richard Rodgers and Carson McCullers and Geoffrey Holder and Santha Rama Rau . . .

"Where's Josh?" Roger Stevens, the co-producer, asked Nedda.

"One hundred two degrees," she said.

He was in bed in his apartment, alone except for the children; he was, for the first time he could remember, sick on opening night. He was very pale and very quiet, and he spoke about a trip to Acapulco that he, Nedda, and the two children would take after Christmas. After that, he was not sure what he wanted to do. There were movies. There were other shows. But he did not know. It had been a tough year, he said.

He went on like this, talking softly, until 11 P.M., when the telephone rang.

"Darling," said Nedda, her voice coming through over the clinking of glasses from Sardi's, "darling, Dick Rodgers wants to speak with you."

"Hello, Josh?"

"Hello, Dick!"

"Now, listen, Josh, this thing you got here tonight, no crap, Josh, it was marvelous!"

Logan seemed unable to speak.

"Really!" Rodgers went on, "I think it's the best job you've done in many years, Josh. It was brilliant! Can't tell you how much I enjoyed it!"

"Oh, Dick"—Logan seemed almost happy enough for tears. "Thank you, Dick . . . thank you . . ."

Then Nedda was back on the phone, then Feibleman, then Oliver Smith, and then others—all saying that the première of *Tiger* was a thing of beauty which the audience loved.

Since there was a New York newspaper strike then, Logan got the reviews over television while sitting in bed: Walter Kerr of the *Herald Tribune* liked some parts, not others; Howard Taubman of the *Times* was ecstatic, giving it possibly his warmest review of the year; the other reviews varied, but one television announcer summed them up as "respectful."

This is all Logan had hoped for. Something respectful. He did not need the big, box-office smash; he'd had plenty of those. And what he *did* want he suspected he might never get.

Well, at least he had stopped being a shit kicker. And— who knows?—soon some new young genius might come up with another *Mister Roberts*.

So Logan settled back in the big bed waiting for Nedda. Three days later he, Nedda, and the children left for Acapulco.

And after thirty-three performances, the play closed.

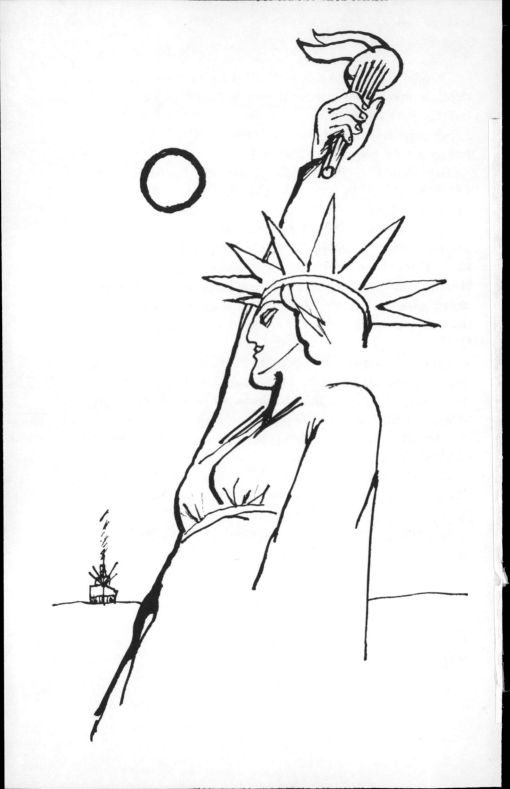

Frank Costello

From the 1880's through the early 1900's they crossed the Atlantic in filthy ships, because they were poor; and dug ditches, because they were ignorant; and hardly a day passed in New York without some Irishman across the street yelling down at them, "Hey, you dirty wop, why don't you go back where you came from?"

They were not from the Italy of da Vinci or the Medicis; they were mostly from Sicily and the South—the Italy of goats and mountain men, and of fat ladies with little mustaches who wore rosaries and black dresses down to their ankles.

They were people who, from pre-Roman times, seemed always to be mourning something: mourning the murders and rapes by the invading Saracens, Greeks, and French; mourning the erupting volcanoes, malaria, taxes, and endless poverty. And, finally, many of them had enough, and they sailed away to America. Two who did this were named Castiglia, and from their town of Cosenza near the toe of Italy they brought their four-year-old son, Francesco, who never dreamed he would someday have an Anglo-Saxon doorman.

He never dreamed that, as Frank Costello, he would someday spend $50 for a hat, $350 for a suit, and be capable of forgetting $27,200 in the back seat of a New York taxicab. Nor did he ever dream that the mere mention of his name would whet the appetites of crime busters, and make thousands of Italian-Americans slightly uncomfortable with *their* names, and hypersensitive to slurs and questions. . . .

> *You Italian?*
> "Half and half."
> *You Italian?*
> "French."
> *You Italian?*
> "None a your goddamn business."

"Hey, wop!"
"Who ya talking to, ya bastid!"

> "And how did you enjoy Rome, Mrs. Winfred?"
> "Fine, except too many Italians."

> "Look, Angelo, my son, don't ever let them push you around because you're Italian. Don't forget that America is named after an Italian, was discovered by an Italian, and Italians were giving art to the world when those god-damned English were living in caves like savages, and painting their faces blue. . . ."

Frank Costello grew up in a New York slum with other peasant children whose parents understood neither the language nor the law. Their mothers relied entirely upon God. And their fathers relied on those better-educated but unreliable countrymen, the *padrones,* with the same blind faith that in later years led them to believe that Primo Carnera would beat Max Baer. These fathers were short and humble men—too short ever to become cops, but just right for collecting garbage and building subways, although some preferred to tend farms upstate, and still others moved into Ohio and Pennsylvania and pushed wheelbarrows filled with rocks up hills to build homes. And when they would reach the top of a certain hill in Ambler, Pennsylvania, panting and sweating, a parrot at the window of a roadside home would shrill down at them: *"Dago-dago-dago-dago-dago-dago-dago!"* The desire to sneak in and murder the parrot at night was strong. But the men never did. Instead at night they drank wine, got sleepy.

Why couldn't you go straight, Frank Costello?
Why couldn't you get a shovel and identify with Christ in Concrete?

He never could. Like many sons of these peasants, Costello despised his father's humility and inadequacy, and sought easy money and escape from his father's grocery stand. In 1908, when he was sixteen and had run away from home and quit school, he was arrested for assault and robbery. In 1912 he was arrested for the same thing. On both occasions he gave his name as Castello. In 1914, when he got his marriage license, he said he was born Costello and was a "plumber" by trade. In 1915, when he served ten months for carrying a concealed weapon, he gave his name as Frank "Saverio" and his occupation as "steamfitter." But when he appeared before General Sessions Court for sentencing, he gave his name as "Stella." He had little capacity for the truth.

By 1923 he was a rum runner; he worked under the notorious ex-longshoreman, Big Bill Dwyer, and helped command a vast operation that illegally shipped liquor down from

Canada via a dozen steel-plated speedboats armed with machine guns, and aided by corrupt Coast Guardsmen. Once Costello's swift vessels accidentally strayed into the path of a speedboat race—swished across the finish line first, and kept going. It was said that during Prohibition the Dwyer-Costello operation not only supplied most of the whisky for the Eastern Seaboard, but also made large shipments to Chicago and throughout the Midwest.

Detectives began to trail Costello. They visited Italian ghettos and asked questions about him. But the neighbors would not talk. Even if a murder had occurred in broad daylight before the eyes of fifty witnesses in that neighborhood, the explanation to the police would have been the same: *"We no see notting."*

These people would no more squeal on a countryman to the New York police in the twenties than they would to the Saracen conquerors in the ninth century, the Byzantine Greeks in the tenth century, or the cruel French in the thirteenth century. Suspicious of all alien authority, they had learned the art of silence—learned it through centuries of biting their lips. The had also learned to accept the worst because the worst had long been their heritage in both Sicily and around Costello's home town of Cosenza. More than 150 landslides were recorded in Cosenza alone in 1903, and almost simultaneously the vicious Phylloxera plant parasite attacked the grapevines of the region's wine makers, and soon Bordeaux monopolized the world's wine market. Malaria was so bad in Cosenza in 1807 that it even wiped out eight hundred of the French soldiers—just as, in 1173, it had eliminated one of Thomas à Becket's fleeing murderers, William de Tracy, and in 410 had cut down Alaric, King of the Visigoths, shortly after he had plundered Rome.

"Were statistics available," wrote historian Norman Douglas of Italy's wildly beautiful South, "I have not the slightest doubt that fever could be shown to be largely responsible for the withering of its spiritual life."

To survive here amid the pestilence, poverty, impossible taxes, and torture, the peasant had to live by his wits, often remain silent, and wait for revenge—as had that vengeful band of Sicilians in 1282 before butchering an entire French garrison after a soldier had raped and murdered a Palermo maiden on her wedding day. It is said that out of this incident, glorified in a Verdi opera, came the inspiration for the Mafia—a union pledged to avenge offenses to a brother, never appeal for police protection, and never, never—on pain of death—to reveal anything about the organization or its membership to the law.

This was Frank Costello's background, and even today a travel book on this poor Southern tip of Italy reads: "While at a hotel or *pension* in Calabria, dispute in 'friendly fashion' every item. It is a matter of principle. By this system, which must not be overdone, your position in the house gradually changes; from being a guest, you become a friend, a brother. For it is your duty to show, above all things, that you are not *scemo*—witless, soft-headed—the unforgivable sin in the South. You may be a forger or cut-throat—why not? It is a vocation like any other. . . ."

And so it was in New York in the twenties that the police encountered silence in Italian Harlem, Brooklyn, and on Mulberry Street in Manhattan. After the police had gone, the men would mutter among themselves, "We wanta no trouble." And they would agree that Costello had done no wrong—the law was merely picking on him because he was Italian. Their obedient wives over the stoves would nod. Then, pushing pasta and wine in front of their husbands, the women would plead, *"Eat-*a, *eat-*a*,"* in their white-washed apartments with madonnas atop the radio, and crosses everywhere. *"Eat-*a*."*

Frank Costello himself felt he had done no wrong. And, in 1925, he became an American citizen. When asked his occupation, he answered, with a straight face and clear voice, "Real estate."

Following Prohibition, Costello's diversified interests included slot machines, gambling, and a legitimate business in the distribution of Scotch whisky. When Mayor Fiorello La Guardia had the New York police junk the slots and dump them at sea, Costello moved machines into New Orleans with the cooperation of Senator Huey Long, who in 1936 said he wished to raise extra money for Louisiana orphans, widows, and the blind. As managers and collectors for his slot machines, Costello hired the two Geigerman boys, his brothers-in-law, both former cab drivers.

"Dudley Geigerman is probably the thriftiest man ever heard of anywhere," wrote one crime reporter. "At a time when he was paying $40 a month rent, buying furniture on the installment plan and worrying about paying a maid $6 a week, he was reporting to the government taxable income of more than $100,000 a year. The suspicious agents of the Internal Revenue Department said it was mostly Costello's money and that Dudley was helping to keep Costello away from the high tax brackets. But they were unable to prove it."

Costello, to be sure, was trying to live a quiet, inconspicuous life during the thirties. The ten months he'd spent in jail in 1915 for carrying a concealed weapon was the first and last time he'd been behind bars. And it was said in his behalf that in 1929, following the St. Valentine's Day massacre in Chicago, Frank Costello convinced a convention of gangsters at Atlantic City of the utter senselessness of carrying weapons and murdering rival gangs. He advocated instead that rival gangs respect one another's territorial rights. As for himself, he dabbled in New York politics and contributed to the campaigns of his favorite politicians. Among the politicians who allegedly visited Costello's penthouse in 1942 was William O'Dwyer, a future Mayor of New York City. But Costello's notoriety was not so well established then. The *New York Times* on July 17, 1942, identified Costello as a "sportsman." He was always polite and entertained graciously at his estate in Long Island. He was also a model husband. He gave his Jewish wife, the former Loretta Geigerman, charge accounts at leading Fifth Avenue shops, and uttered nary a word when she spent $241.91 for three hats and a handkerchief at Mr. John, Inc.

Thousands of dollars were given by Costello to charities, churches, and an endless procession of panhandlers. But he did not worry; he had money coming in from all sides. He was even listed as earning an $18,000-a-year salary from his work with Dandy Phil Kastel at the Beverly Club, a Louisiana restaurant and gambling house, although nobody knew precisely what Costello's job was.

"And what did you do for that salary, Mr. Costello?" a crime committeeman asked in a later investigation.

"Well," Costello said, "I helped to get different acts, and I solicited some business. In other words, if someone was going to Louisiana, I would recommend a place. I was just a goodwill man for them. And I would recommend different acts for the club."

"How did you go about looking for acts?"

"Well," he said, "if I would hear of a good act, I would go in there, have dinner, and watch it. If I thought it was good, I would call them up and say, 'Here is a good act.' "

"What acts did you recommend?"

"Well, Joe Louis, Sophie Tucker, and a lot of big acts."

"Would it take an expert to recommend headliners like that to a night club?"

"Yes, well, I don't consider myself an expert. But a good act can go bad, too. No material, they would go bad. If they have new material, you will recommend it."

"Did you do anything about preparing or reviewing the material of these acts?"

"No. I was just soliciting them. Then, if I would like them, I told them I liked them."

"And for that you got $18,000 a year?"

"That's right."

Frank Costello had them completely baffled. "Costello," wrote Herbert Asbury, "has succeeded in becoming as mysterious a figure as the American underworld has ever produced. Not that the cops, both city and Federal, haven't tried to find out. They've been trying, in fact, since the middle 1920's, but by and large Costello has been too clever; they've been led up so many blind alleys that he has become a symbol of frustration to policemen and G-men throughout the country."

Costello's telephone wires were tapped by the F.B.I.; the Federal Bureau of Narcotics printed his photo on its black list; Mayor La Guardia called him a "bum." But Costello, who never kept less than $50,000 in cash in his apartment on Central Park West, paid other hoods to do his chores. Somehow he remained clean, even though New York detectives trailed him throughout the city: into the Waldorf, where he often lunched with politicians and the finest people; into the steambaths at the Biltmore, where he sweated it out in the same room with James A. Farley, Hank Greenberg, Gene

Tunney, Bernard Gimbel, and dozens of distinguished executives; into barbershops, where he was fawned upon, manicured, powdered, and surrounded by serfs who fell over themselves for the big tip; through Central Park, where they observed the stocky, well-tailored figure of Costello observing the wonders of nature, studying the sky, watching animals behind bars in the park's zoo; and then to the Wollman Memorial rink, about which a *New York Times*man wrote: "The Wollman Memorial rink in Central Park . . . has attracted a good many celebrities, including Frank Costello, the gambler, of whom it is reported that he did not skate, but merely looked on skeptically, grunted and walked away."

As for the other immigrants, life became a little better through the 1930's and into the 1940's. The parrot who shrilled "dago-dago-dago-dago-dago" in Ambler, Pennsylvania, was dead. There was much to cheer about. The DiMaggio brothers could do no wrong. Pinza was sensational. And Valli became the first Italian movie actress on the American screen with something more than just large breasts. In Manhattan, The Lambs Club, in a moment of magnanimity, honored its long-time bootblack, Biaggio Velluzzi, with a dinner and theatre tickets. Biaggio, known to all as "Murph," said, "Those-a Lambs a-lovea me, and I a-lovea those-a Lambs."

All around the nation, the sons of wheelbarrow pushers and bricklayers were prospering in their own construction firms. Former caddies were being promoted to club professionals, and were able to strut around country clubs on Sunday afternoons in white yachting jackets—and *sign* for their drinks. Italian-American schoolboys still were conscious of their long names, and perhaps even envied the shorter names of Negroes, but relatively few Italians changed them; it was a matter of family pride. Or a matter of realizing that changing names would fool nobody. Perhaps a lesson had been learned from the old Italian prizefighter, Joseph Carrora, who changed his name to Johnny Dundee, but was from then on called the "Scotch Wop."

World War II produced such heralded, but short-lived heroes as the ace pilot Captain Don Gentile; and Army life brought to many Italian-American boys a sense of belonging to something more than just a Catholic parish, a labor union, or a Brooklyn bowling team sponsored by an olive-oil importer.

"It's a funny thing," said Corporal DiAngelo of Ralph Avenue, Brooklyn, "but when we moved up into Naples and Rome, all the Italians there called me an *Americano*. It was the first time in my life I'd ever felt American before. . . ."

And finally, the sons of these Sicilian and Southern immigrants, some of whose parents had posed in 1910 for Jacob Riis's forlorn photos of Mulberry Street, were moving up in politics—some with Costello's help, and some with help from the large Italian-American voting bloc. Thus, in this era of American history, there existed a generation of politicians who were never quite sure whether they were elected *because* they were Italian, or *despite* it.

Nevertheless, it felt good to sit on a judicial bench and act like a priest in a long, black gown. And it was good, as an Assemblyman, to kiss the wife and kids good-bye and ride the trains to the state capital. Although, in their shiny dark suits, pointed black shoes, white-on-white shirts, and Windsor-knot ties, these politicians were rarely mistaken for Choate men.

Frank Costello's personal ambition during these years was respectability. And this seemed almost attainable in 1949 when he was asked to serve as vice-chairman of a Salvation Army fund-raising drive. Walter Hoving, president of Tiffany and then chairman of the committee, wrote Costello that "key people in New York" were being sought and that the committee was "most anxious" to have Mr. Costello's help.

Delighted and flattered, Costello showed the letter to his attorney, George Wolf. Wolf thought there had been a mistake. He called the committee and asked, "Do you know who this man Costello is? He's a former bootlegger."

Wolf recalled that the Salvation Army was fully aware of Costello's former occupation, but nonetheless would be "delighted" with any help he could give. So Costello threw a $100-a-plate party at the Copacabana and invited, among others, Manhattan Borough President Hugo E. Rogers, and many Supreme Court Justices and leading New York politicians. He was able to collect $3,500 from contributions this way and, adding $6,500 of his own money, sent $10,000 to the Salvation Army.

But when the newspapers learned of the party, and printed the names of those present, it became a *cause célèbre*. Those in attendance came off badly, it being inferred that they were Costello's pawns. Costello looked worse, and the indignant public's response made it mandatory that action be taken.

Frank Costello, seeing his public relations drive shattered, became so annoyed with the publicity that, according to Warren Moscow, writing in the Sunday *New York Times,* Costello "arranged for the ouster of Hugo E. Rogers as leader of Tammany Hall, and for the selection of Carmine G. De Sapio as his successor. He hoped that De Sapio would make a good, respectable leader, that the public would forget about Costello while Costello enjoyed his golf and his friends in respectable retirement, free from politics and racket connections." But Mr. Moscow continued, "The Senate Crime Investigation Committee in 1951 insisted on raking up Costello's past, even after his plea, at the start of the hearings, that 'I am only asking you to respect fundamental rights and principles, I am begging you to treat me as a human being.' "

So Frank Costello went before the committee. And when he insisted that his face not be exposed on television, the cameras focused on his fingers, which tapped and danced nervously, offering a grotesque ballet for the home-screen audience. For hours he sat under the questioning with the cameras nipping away at his fingers, and one evening he was promised a large sum by cigarette salesmen if he would display their brand of cigarettes before the camera. But Costello, ever loyal to English Ovals, refused. Yet he was sick of the exposure even to his fingers, and sick in the throat, too, he told the committee.

"For a sick man," the counsel retorted, "Mr. Costello is a very astute witness."

"When I testify," Costello said hoarsely, "I want to testify truthfully, and my mind don't function."

In addition to being a reluctant witness, Costello had also become short-tempered and listless.

"Mr. Costello," shouted the counsel, finally, "did you hear the testimony . . ."

Costello's gray eyes blazed; his steel-gray hair around his temples bristled. "I am not going to answer another question," he said, firmly. "I am going to walk out."

Behind his attorney, Frank Costello moved toward the exit, disappeared, and made page 1 headlines:

COSTELLO DEFIES SENATORS,

WALKS OUT OF HEARING HERE;

FACES ARREST ON CONTEMPT

Pleads Ill Health

LIGHTS AND CAMERAS BAR

PROPER TESTIMONY, HIS

ATTORNEYS SAY

Walking out was unwise; he had gone too far. He had done it before a national television audience, and the Senate could never condone such public defiance. Costello was quickly found guilty of contempt and sentenced to eighteen months in jail.

But even in jail Costello baffled the law. He continued to smoke English Ovals, although nobody knew how he smuggled them in. He ate steak—ebony on the outside, claret on the inside, just as he'd ordered them at "21"—and yet it was impossible to uncover the source of the steaks. The unbelievable power that Costello was able to wield despite his imprisonment was demonstrated some years later when he performed a behind-bars miracle for his attorney, Edward Bennett Williams.

Williams, during a visit to Costello's jail, seemed concerned about something, and Costello, detecting it, asked, "What's bothering you, Mr. Williams?"

Williams explained that he and his wife were taking her parents out that night to celebrate their thirty-fifth wedding anniversary, and that he had promised them tickets to *My Fair Lady;* but the particular agent who had promised Williams the tickets—a person who'd always been reliable in the past—had suddenly failed on this occasion.

"Mr. Williams," Costello said, "you shoulda told me; maybe I coulda helped."

Williams admitted it had never occurred to him that a man in jail could help get four tickets at the last minute to a hit Broadway show.

Costello shrugged.

It was then 5 P.M.

When Williams returned to his hotel room, he heard a soft rap on the door. Upon opening it, a broad-shouldered man under a slouch hat grunted something, handed over an envelope containing four tickets to that evening's performance of *My Fair Lady,* then quickly disappeared down the hall.

While Costello was in jail, the grandchildren of the immigrants were growing up and becoming aware of the subtle handicaps of their names, and becoming confused by some conflicts in their environment. What these children heard at home often differed from what they read in books by non-Italians, heard in church from Irish priests, learned in schools under Protestant deans, culled from editorials by Jewish liberals, and overheard on streets. . . .

"Those Italians, they're all alike. . . ." "Why don't they ship Costello back where . . ."

And among Italians they heard . . .

"They're picking on Costello 'cause he's . . ."

"God, if they pulled that stuff on the Jews, the Anti-Defamation League would . . ."

Frank Costello rarely defended himself verbally. To newsmen's questions on how he made so much money, his stock answers usually were either "No comment" or "I don't sell Bibles." Although he once explained to a reporter, "Look, I'm a gambler, but I don't operate where I'm not wanted."

No sooner had he completed his year in prison for contempt than he was hauled back on charges of tax evasion. His high-priced attorneys tried hard to beat the case in court.

"Now for God's sake, Frank," one of them said, "when you appear in court tomorrow don't come in wearing one of your $350 suits, and appear so affluent."

"What do you want me to wear?" Costello asked.

"What you have on," the attorney said, nodding toward Costello's blue denim prison suit.

Costello thought it over for a second, then frowned and

said, "I'm sorry, but I'd rather blow the goddamn case."

He did. On May 14, 1954, the headlines read: "Costello Guilty in Tax Fraud Case!" And the newspapers and magazines ran a photograph of Costello that was like so many other photos of him during his career: it showed him coming down the steps of the courthouse flanked by lawyers, his gray eyes lowered, his gray fedora squarely on his head, his nose long and rounded, his sullen face sucking in on a cigarette, his expression giving no clue as to how he felt or what he thought.

Before getting into an automobile on this May morning, he turned to reporters on the sidewalk and said, "I think this is a political thing. A lot of guys trying to get ahead by climbing on my back. And that's the way the world goes."

"What was the first mistake?" Walter Winchell asked.

"If you call it a mistake," Costello said, "I guess it was being born of poor parents and raised in a tough neighborhood. If things had been different I might have gone to college and been sitting up there with Mr. Kefauver. But I can say honestly that since I got old enough to know right from wrong I've tried to live a good life. I've been married to the same girl for thirty-five years. How many of my critics can match that?"

In 1956, rather than continue on in jail, Frank Costello volunteered to go into exile if the government would nullify his jail sentence. He might have even returned to Cosenza. But the Justice Department refused.

If Costello had been able to return, however, he would have encountered a lovely but mysterious land still in the Dark Ages—just as he'd left it when he was four, and just as it had been hundreds of years before his birth. He would have seen peasant women walking along the roads around Cosenza

*balancing clay pots on their heads. And the men riding don-
keys there would have sun-baked, Biblical faces. He would
have seen small, ancient white houses of stone studded in the
vast green mountainside to the east, and to the west, in the
blue-green Tyrrhenian Sea, swarthy boys would be swimming
in the nude and making obscene gestures to the trains that
passed.*

*Frank Costello would probably not have liked this land; it
is not pleasant to see one's roots so exposed, nor to be reminded of such humble beginnings. If Costello were there, he
would see few American tourists—except a few second-gen-
eration Italian-Americans who might now be of age to travel
and visit any relatives in the South or to see the birthplace of
their grandparents.*

*And every once in a while Frank Costello might hear a
young grandson being greeted at the Cosenza train station by
packs of jubilant relatives who would make the boy feel like
a new Messiah, or a kind of Latin Lindbergh in a ticker-tape
parade—except instead of confetti, the boy would be show-
ered with wet kisses from endless uncles, aunts, and cousins
who could not understand a word of English.*

*Nevertheless, with an 8-mm movie camera the boy would
begin to click off scenes of these relatives in Costello country,
and the films perhaps later would be shown in a kitchen back
in Brooklyn where a bedsheet, serving as a projection screen,
would be tacked to the flowered wallpaper. And when the
lights would go on in this Brooklyn kitchen, tears would be
seen in the eyes of some of the older people seated around the
room. . . .*

In the latter part of 1956, after Edward Bennett Williams
proved that the conviction had been based on illegal wiretap

evidence, the gambler got out of jail for a while, and tried very hard to avoid publicity. But he was back in the nation's headlines soon because on the night of May 2, 1957, at 10:55 o'clock, as Costello was walking past his Anglo-Saxon doorman toward his penthouse apartment, a bullet whizzed toward his head, nicked his scalp, and whistled through his $50 gray fedora.

Frank Costello insisted to the police that he had no idea who did the shooting.

"Isn't it a fact, Mr. Costello, that you saw this man?" a detective asked. "Isn't it a fact?"

"No, I haven't seen no man."

"Do you know of any reason why anybody in the wide world should want to kill you, Mr. Costello?"

"No, I don't know of any human being that had a motive."

This was *typical* Costello cooperation, the investigators agreed. But Frederic Sondhern, Jr., the writer and Mafia expert, pointed out that Costello's silence was merely his adherence to the Mafia law prohibiting squealing on a countryman. And after the trial Mr. Sondhern quoted a Federal official as saying that Costello, faithful to his tradition, now saw himself as a "good soldier" from the Mafioso's viewpoint. "He'd be committing treason, high treason, by going over to the enemy, which is the way Costello sees us," the officer said. "He might be executed at the end of a .38, but he would certainly be punished by something which to him seems even worse—ostracism and the contempt of the brothers, who are the only people that he really knows. You've just seen the Mafia's *omertà* (silence) working, my friend; it's more than a code or a pattern of faith. It's almost a religion—with teeth in it."

Because Costello refused to cooperate, and refused to

answer questions about certain numbers on slips of paper found in his pockets on the night he was shot, he was adjudged in contempt. And soon Costello was not only back in jail, but was also being divested of his citizenship on the grounds that, when he was naturalized in 1925 and was asked his occupation, he said "Real estate." He should have said "Bootlegging."

The deportation proceedings were protested throughout Italy.

"Why should he be deported to *Italy?*" they asked. "He is not Italian—he is a product of the corrupt American civilization!" The newspaper *Il Secolo D'Italia* called it a curious punishment—sending a man back to a country whose language he does not speak. The Italian government did not mind taking credit for such well-bred Italian-Americans as Vicenzo Botta, vice-president of the exclusive Union League Club from 1863 to 1894; or Count Luigi Palma di Cesnola, a Yankee general in the Civil War; or the scientist Enrico Fermi; or any of those thousands of other Italian immigrants who made good in America, and seemed to confirm the view that Italians, after all, are extremely cultured and attractive people—whether one regards them in their Roman role as conquerors, or their Renaissance role as artists, or in their post–World War II role as cosmopolites driving Ferrari sports cars, or wearing Simonetta gowns, or playing in Fellini films, or carrying Gucci handbags, or pounding Olivetti typewriters, or . . .

But when it came to taking credit for those unskilled Sicilian or Southern Italian peasants whose offspring became gangsters, the Italian government became very, very sensitive. And who could blame it? There seemed to be so many Italian gangsters in the United States. . . .

"That's a lie!" shouted former Congressman Alfred E. Santangelo of New York. "And I have figures to prove it." Recent figures from the six major prisons in the United States show that of 23,605 inmates, only 588 had Italian-sounding names, and the average prison population of those with Italian ancestry is 2.5 percent, Santangelo said. He had gathered these figures to support his demand that the ABC-TV show *The Untouchables* stop giving Italian-sounding names to the fictional criminal characters on the show. *"The Untouchables* is disgraceful," he said. "Kids were calling it *The Italian Family Hour* and saying, 'Let's go watch the Cops and Wops on teevee.' "

Mr. Santangelo, supported by many Italian-American organizations, protested the insults to Italian names, and enough pressure was put on ABC's sponsors, Liggett & Myers, to force a change in the script.

This is the big difference in the Italian-American of today —he is quick to defend himself, whereas his grandfather, who was illiterate, couldn't; and his father, often insecure, wouldn't. The evidence of this change in the present Italo-American generation's behavior can be found in such news items as:

New York Times—The Italian-American League Against Discrimination announced yesterday that it would seek to counteract by publicity campaigns recent tendencies to characterize Italians as criminals. . . .

UPI—The weekly newspaper, *The Pilot,* said in its lead editorial that there are also gangsters who are English, Irish, Dutch, Jewish, German, Negro. . . .

New York *Post*—Frank Sinatra almost came to blows with Desi Arnaz in an argument over the way Italians are depicted in some TV shows. . . . The result is that Sinatra moved his TV company out of the Desilu studios and into the Sam Goldwyn studios. . . .

Today the offspring of the immigrants who came to America at the turn of the century are gaining the respectability that eluded Frank Costello. Like the peasant Irish before them, the peasant Italian's sons and grandsons are leaving the labor class and are moving into white-collared security: they are Civil Service workers, CPA's, they're solid union musicians—and their music is not "far out." These products of peasants try hard *not* to be different in America. They keep one foot on the bag, play it safe.

Many have switched from white-on-white shirts to Oxford buttondowns, and have become aware of the hazards of garlic. On Sundays many of them drive to golf courses in long, low automobiles with plastic Christ figures on the dashboard. Some have daughters who, when they become engaged, will have a photo by Bachrach. They are not hungry enough to make good prizefighters any more; Marciano was the last of the great Italian heavyweights. They are successful as advertising and news writers, yet have established no literary tradition in the English language, and there is not a good novelist among them. On the radio and television they sing soft, soothing melodies, but most of the great opera voices are still imported. The Italo-Americans have not yet *arrived,* like the Irish, but the Italian masses are on the rise—aspiring to solid, middle-class status. Great numbers of them have moved out of the neighborhoods of their parents, and become "integrated." Quite a few have left the city altogether for suburban living. And when asked why they left the city, some become almost indignant, and exclaim, "What! And live next to the *Puerto Ricans!*"

Meanwhile, as Frank Costello approaches his seventy-fourth birthday, the present-generation Italians are celebrating his decline, in a sense, because his notoriety reminds them of an era they wish to forget. Costello never understood the rules of the New World because he was influenced by the tradition of a land that exists in the past. When he left it for America, and crossed the Atlantic in two weeks, he actually was crossing hundreds of years of civilization. He was moving into a world in which Robin Hoods were out of date. He was moving into a land that possessed hostility toward the most-recently-arrived peasant. While most immigrants accepted their lowly status, and worked patiently to overcome it, Costello did not.

He rebelled early against the society that called him "wop." His father, who might have dominated family life in Italy—as fathers do there—was illiterate and incapable here. His father was *scemo*—the unforgivable sin of the Southern peasant and Sicilian. Costello had no respect for him. At sixteen he ran away from his home in the slum and regarded those who were not his friends as Saracens. He justified his thievery by his kindness to his wife, and by giving money to panhandlers and for stained glass windows to churches.

And he will die thinking he has done no wrong.

TRAVELING

II

LIGHT

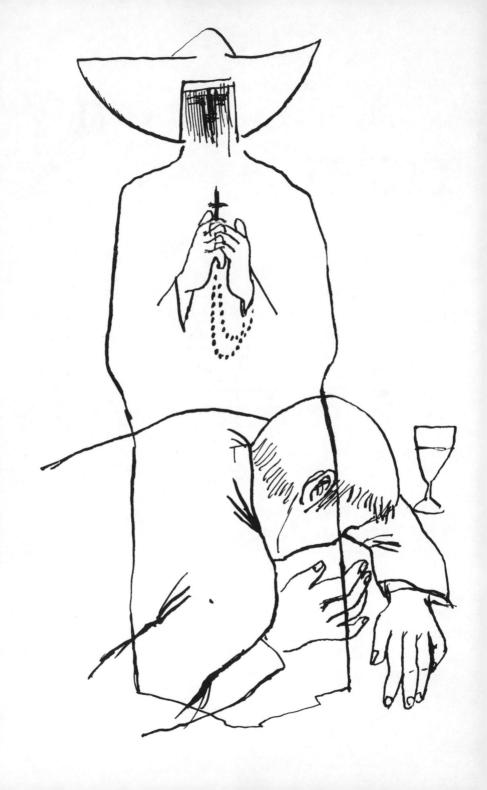

Flying to Dublin with Peter O'Toole

All the children in the classroom had their pencils out and were drawing horses, as the nun had instructed—all, that is, except one little boy who, having finished, was sitting idly behind his desk.

"Well," the nun said, looking down at his horse, "why not draw something else—a saddle, or something?"

A few minutes later she returned to see what he had drawn. Suddenly her face was scarlet. The horse now had a penis and was urinating in the pasture.

Wildly, with both hands, the nun began to flail the boy. Then other nuns rushed in and they, too, flailed him, knocking him to the floor, and not listening as he sobbed, bewilderedly, "But, but . . . I was only drawing what I saw . . . only drawing what I saw!"

"Oh, those bitches!" said Peter O'Toole, now thirty-one, still feeling the sting after all these years. "Those destitute, old unmarried birds with those withered, sexless hands! God, how I hated those nuns!"

He threw his head back, finished his Scotch, then asked the

stewardess for another. Peter O'Toole was sitting in an airplane that one hour before had left London, where he has long lived in exile, and was flying to Ireland, his birthplace. The plane was filled with businessmen and rosy-cheeked Irishwomen, and also a scattering of priests, one of whom held a cigarette in what seemed to be a long, thin pair of wire tweezers—presumably so he would not touch tobacco with fingers that would later hold the Sacrament.

O'Toole, unaware of the priest, smiled as the stewardess brought his drink. She was a floridly robust little blonde in a tight green tweed uniform.

"Oh, look at that ass," O'Toole said softly, shaking his head, raising his eyes with approval. "That ass is covered with tweed made in Connemara, where I was born. . . . Nicest asses in the world, Ireland. Irishwomen still are carrying water on their heads and carrying their husbands home from pubs, and such things are the greatest posture builders in the world."

He sipped his Scotch and looked out the window. The plane was now descending, and through the clouds he could see the soft, verdant fields, the white farmhouses, the gentle hills of outer Dublin, and he said he felt, as returning Irishmen often do, both some sadness and some joy. They are sad at seeing again what it was that forced them to leave, and feel some guilt, too, for having left though they know they could never have fulfilled their dreams amid all this poverty and strangling strictness; yet they are happy because Ireland's beauty seems imperishable, unchanged from the time of their childhood, and thus each trip back home to Ireland is a blissful reunion with youth.

Though Peter O'Toole remains an uprooted Irishman by choice, he leaves London and returns to Ireland every now and then to do some drinking, to play the horses at the

Punchestown racetrack outside Dublin, and to spend some solitary hours thinking. He had had very little time for private thinking recently; there had been those grueling two years in the desert with *Lawrence of Arabia,* and then starring on the London stage in Bertold Brecht's *Baal,* and then co-starring with Richard Burton in the film, *Becket,* and then he would star in *Lord Jim,* with other films to follow.

Big money was rolling in now, for the first time in his life. He had just bought a nineteen-room house in London, and finally was able to afford paintings by Jack B. Yeats. Yet O'Toole was no more contented or secure now than he had been as an underfed drama student living on a barge, a barge that sank one night after too many people had come to a party.

He could still be wild and self-destructive, and the psychiatrists had been no help. All he knew was that within him, simmering in the smithy of his soul, were confusion and conflict, and they were probably responsible for his talent, his rebellion, his exile, his guilt. They were all linked somehow with Ireland and the Church, with his smashing up so many cars that his license had to be taken away, and with marching in Ban-the-Bomb parades, with becoming obsessed with Lawrence of Arabia, with detesting cops, barbed wire, and girls who shave under their arms; with being an esthete, a horse player, a former altar boy, a drinker who now wanders through the streets at night buying the same book ("My life is littered with copies of *Moby Dick"*) and reading the same sermon in that book (". . . and if we obey God, we must disobey ourselves . . ."); with being gentle, generous, sensitive, yet suspicious ("You're talking to an Irish bookie's son; you can't con me!"); with devotion to his wife, loyalty to old friends, great concern over the uncertain eyesight of his three-year-old daughter, now wearing very thick glasses ("Daddy, Daddy! I broke my eyes!" "Don't cry, Kate, don't cry—we'll get you a new pair"); with theatrical genius that is equally moving whether performing pantomime or Hamlet; with an anger that can be sudden ("Why should I tell *you* the truth? Who are you, Bertrand Russell?") and with anger that quickly subsides ("Look, I'd tell you if I knew why, but I don't know, just don't know . . ."); and with the as yet unrealized contradictions in the Peter O'Toole who, at this very moment, was about to land in Ireland . . . where he was born thirty-one years ago . . . where he would have his next drink.

Two bumps, and the plane was safely down, racing across the concrete, then spinning around and rolling toward the Dublin air terminal. When the door was opened, a crowd of photographers and reporters moved in, flash bulbs fixed, and soon they were popping away as Peter O'Toole, a thin, lanky man of six feet three inches, wearing a green corduroy jacket, a green bowtie, and green socks (he wears nothing *but* green socks, even with tuxedos) came down the steps, smiling and waving in the sun. He posed for pictures, gave a radio interview, bought everybody a drink; he laughed and back-slapped, he was charming and suave, he was his public self, his airport self.

Then he got into a limousine that would take him into the city, and soon he was riding through the narrow, winding roads past the farmhouses, past the goats and cows and green, very green land stretching for miles in the distance.

"A lovely land," O'Toole said, with a sigh. "God, you can love it! But you can't live in it. It's a frightening thing. My father, who lives in England, won't put a foot in Ireland any more. And yet, you mention one word against Ireland and he goes stark raving mad. . . .

"Oh, Ireland," O'Toole went on, "it's the sow that ate its own farrow. Tell me one Irish artist that ever produced here, just one! God, Jack Yeats couldn't sell a painting in this country, and *all the talent* . . . oh, daddy . . . You know what Ireland's biggest export is? It's men. Men . . . Shaw, Joyce, Synge, they couldn't stay here. O'Casey couldn't stay. Why? Because O'Casey preaches the Doctrine of Joy, daddy, that's why. . . . Oh, the Irish know despair, *by God they do!* They are Dostoyevskian about it. But Joy, dear love, in *this* land! . . . Oh, dear Father," O'Toole went on, pounding his breast, "forgive me, Father, for I have f——ed Mrs. Rafferty. . . . Ten Hail Marys, son, five Our Fathers . . . But Father, Father, I didn't enjoy f——ing Mrs. Rafferty. . . . Good, son, *good* . . .

"Ireland," O'Toole repeated, "you can love it . . . can't *live* in it."

Now he was at the hotel. It was near the Liffey River not far from the tower described by Joyce in *Ulysses*. O'Toole had a drink at the bar. He seemed very quiet and somber, so different from the way he had been at the airport.

"The Celts are, at rock bottom, deep pessimists," Peter O'Toole said, tossing down his Scotch. Part of his own pessimism, he added, springs from his birthplace, Connemara, "the wildest part of Ireland, famine country, a land without horizons"—a land that Jack Yeats paints so well into his Irish faces, faces that remind O'Toole so much of his seventy-five-year-old father, Patrick O'Toole, a former bookmaker, a dashing gentleman, tall and very slim, like Peter; who nearly always drank too much and fought with the police, like Peter; and who was not very lucky at the racetrack, like Peter; and people in the neighborhood back in Connemara used to shake their heads for Patty O'Toole's wife, Constance ("a saint"), and would say, "Oh, what would Patty O'Toole ever do without Connie?"

"When my father would come home from the track after a good day," said Peter O'Toole, leaning against the bar, "the whole room would light up; it was fairyland. But when he lost, it was black. In our house, it was always either a wake . . . or a wedding."

Later in his boyhood, Peter O'Toole was taken out of Ireland; his father, wishing to be closer to the racetracks clustered in northern England's industrial district, moved the family to Leeds, a slum of one-down, two-up houses.

"My first memory of Leeds as a child was being lost," said Peter O'Toole, tossing down another drink. "I remember wandering around the city . . . remember seeing a man painting a telephone pole *green* . . . And I remember him going away and leaving his paint brushes and things behind. . . . And I remember finishing the pole for him. . . . And I remember being brought to the police station. . . . And remember looking up at the desk, all white tile, white as a nun's hand, and then I remember seeing a big, f——ing nasty looking down at me. . . ."

At thirteen, Peter O'Toole had quit school and had gone to work briefly in a warehouse and learned to break string without scissors, a talent he has never lost, and after that he worked as a copyboy and photographer's assistant at the *Yorkshire Evening News,* a job he liked very much until it occurred to him that newspapermen remain primarily along the sidelines of life recording the deeds of famous men, and rarely become famous themselves, and he very much wanted to become famous, he said. At eighteen years of age, he had copied in his notebook the lines that would be his credo, and now, in this bar in Dublin, tilting back on his barstool, he recited them aloud:

"I do not choose to be a common man . . . it is my right to be uncommon—if I can. . . . I seek opportunity—not security. . . . I want to take the calculated risk; to dream and to build, to fail and to succeed . . . to refuse to barter incentive for a dole. . . . I prefer the challenges of life to the guaranteed existence, the thrill of fulfillment to the stale calm of utopia. . . ."

After he finished, two drunken men at the far end of the bar clapped their hands, and O'Toole bought them, and himself, another drink.

His career as an actor, he said, began after his tour in the Navy and a year of study at the Royal Academy of Dramatic Art. One of his first acting jobs was with the Bristol Old Vic Company impersonating a Georgian peasant in a Chekhov play.

"I was supposed to lumber onto the stage and say, 'Dr. Ostroff, the horses have arrived,' and then walk off," O'Toole said. "But not *me*. I decided this Georgian peasant was really *Stalin!* And so I played it with a slight limp, like Stalin's, and fixed my make-up like Stalin . . . and when I came on the stage, smoldering with resentment for the aristocracy, I could hear a hush come over the audience. Then I glared at Dr. Ostroff . . . and said, 'Dr. Horsey, the Ostroffs have arrived!' "

In the next three years at the Bristol Old Vic, he played seventy-three roles, including Hamlet, but, until he got the movie role in *Lawrence of Arabia*, nobody had heard of Peter O'Toole, said Peter O'Toole, his voice hard.

"Lawrence!" O'Toole spat out, swallowing his Scotch. "I became obsessed by that man, and it was bad. A true artist should be able to jump into a bucket of shit and come out smelling of violets, but I spent two years and three months making that picture, and it was two years, three months of thinking about nothing *but* Lawrence, and you were him, and that's how it was day after day, day after day, and it became bad for me, personally, and it killed my acting later.

"After Lawrence, as you know, I did *Baal* and a close friend of mine, after my dress rehearsal, came back and said, 'What's the matter, Peter, what *is* it?' I asked what the hell he meant, and he said, 'There's no *give!*' . . . Christ, his words struck terror in me. Oh, it was bad acting! I was looking at the floor . . . couldn't get my voice going again. . . . I was flabby, diffuse. . . . Later I said, 'You're in trouble, daddy,' and I felt it in my f——ing toes. I was emotionally bankrupt after that picture.

"On a BBC show, on Harry Craig's show—that mother dug too deep!—I said that after *Lawrence* I was afraid of being mutilated. That filming for that length of time, two years, three months, and having all the responsibility for the performance but none of the control . . . Christ, in one scene of the film I saw a close-up of my face when I was twenty-seven years old, and then, eight seconds later, there was another close-up of me when I was twenty-nine years old! *Eight goddamn seconds* and two years of my life had gone from me!

"Oh, it's painful seeing it all there on a screen, solidified, embalmed," he said, staring straight ahead toward the rows of bottles. "Once a thing is solidified it stops being a living thing. That's why I love the theatre. It's the Art of the Moment. I'm in love with ephemera and I hate permanence. Acting is making words into flesh, and I love classical acting because . . . because you need the vocal range of an opera singer . . . the movement of a ballet dancer . . . you have to be able to *act* . . . it's turning your whole body into a musical instrument on which you yourself play. . . . It's more than behaviorism, which is what you get in the movies. . . . Chrissake, what *are* movies anyway? Just f——ing moving photographs, that's all. But the theatre! Ah, there you have the *impermanence* that I love. It's a reflection of life somehow. It's . . . it's . . . like building a statue of snow. . . ."

Peter O'Toole looked at his watch. Then he paid the barman and waved good-bye to the drunks in the corner. It was 1:15 P.M.—time to be getting to the track.

The chauffeur, a fat and quiet man who had been dozing in the hotel lobby all this time, woke up when he heard O'Toole singing and sauntering out of the bar, and he quickly hopped up when O'Toole announced cheerfully, bowing slightly, "To the races, m'good man."

In the car on the way to Punchestown, O'Toole, who was in good spirits but not drunk by any means, recalled the joy he'd had as a boy when his father would take him to the race track. Sometimes, O'Toole said, his father would miscalculate the odds at his bookie stand, or would lose so heavily on one of his own bets that he would not have enough cash to pay off his winning customers; so, immediately after the race was over, but before the customers could charge toward the O'Toole bookie booth, Patrick O'Toole would grab Peter's hand and say, "C'm'on, son, let's be off!"—and the two of them would slip through the shrubbery and disappear quickly from the track, and could not return again for a long time.

Punchestown's grandstand was jammed with people when

O'Toole's chauffeur drove toward the clubhouse. There were long lines of people waiting to buy tickets, too, well-dressed people in tweed suits and tweed caps, or Tyrolean hats with feathers sticking up. Beyond the people was the paddock, a paddock of soft, very green grass on which the horses pounded back and forth, circling and turning, nostrils flaring. And behind the paddock, making lots of noise, were rows and rows of bookies, all of them elderly men wearing caps and standing behind their brightly-painted wooden stands, all of them echoing the odds and waving little pieces of paper in the breeze.

Peter O'Toole watched them for a moment, silently. Then, suddenly, a woman's voice could be heard calling, "PEE-*tah,* Pee-*tah,* Pee-*tah* O'Toole, well, how *ah* you?"

O'Toole recognized the woman as one of Dublin society, a well-built woman of about forty whose husband owned race horses and lots of stock in Guinness.

O'Toole smiled and held her hand for a few moments, and she said, "Oh, you look better every day, Pee-tah, even better than you did on those bloody Arab camels. Come to our trailer behind the clubhouse and have drinks with us, dear, won't you?"

O'Toole said he would, but first wanted to place a bet.

He placed a five-pound bet on a horse in the first race but, before the horse could clear the final hedge, the rider was thrown. O'Toole lost the next five races, too, and the liquor was also getting to him. Between races he'd stopped in at the Guinness trailer, a big white van filled with rich men and champagne and elegant Irishwomen who brushed up very close to him, called him "Pee-tah" and saying he should come back to Ireland more often, and, as he smiled and put his long arms around them, he sometimes found that he was leaning on them for support.

Just before the final race, O'Toole wandered out into the fresh air and sun and placed a ten-pound bet on a horse about which he knew nothing; then, instead of going back into the Guinness van, he leaned against the rail near the track, his bloodshot blue eyes gazing at the row of horses lined up at the gate. The bell sounded, and O'Toole's horse, a big chestnut gelding, pulled out ahead, and, swinging around the turn, kicking divots of grass into the air, it maintained the lead, leaped over a hedge, pounded onward, leaped over another hedge, still ahead by two lengths. Now Peter O'Toole began to wake up, and seconds later he was waving his fist in the air, cheering and jumping, as the horse moved across the finish line—and galloped past, the jockey leaning up on the saddle, an easy victor.

"Pee-tah, Pee-tah, you've won!" came the cries from the van.

"Pee-tah, darling, let's have a drink!"

But Peter O'Toole was not interested in a drink. He rushed immediately to the ticket window before the bookie could get away. O'Toole got his money.

After the races, with the late afternoon sun going down and the air suddenly chilly, O'Toole decided he would avoid the parties in Dublin; instead he asked the chauffeur to take him to Glendalough, a quiet, beautiful, almost deserted spot along a lake between two small mountains in outer Dublin, not far from where the earliest O'Tooles were buried, and where he, as a boy, used to take long walks.

By 5:30 P.M. the driver was edging the big car around the narrow dirt roads at the base of the mountain, then he stopped, there being no more road. O'Toole got out, lifted the collar of his green corduroy jacket, and began to walk up the mountain, a bit uneasily, because he was still slightly dazed by all the drinking.

"Oh, Christ, what color!" he shouted, his voice echoing through the valley. "Just look at those trees, those young trees—they're *running*, for chrissake, they're not planted there—and they're so luscious, like pubic hair, and that *lake,* no fish in *that* lake! And no birds sing, it's so quiet, no birds singing in Glendalough on account of there being no fish . . . for them to sing for. . . ."

Then he slumped down on the side of the mountain, tossed his head back against the grass. Then he held his hands in the air, and said, "See that? See that right hand?" He turned his right hand back and forth, saying, "Look at those scars, daddy," and there were about thirty or forty little scars inside his right hand as well as on his knuckles, and his little finger was deformed.

"I don't know if there's any significance to it, daddy, but . . . but *I am a left-hander who was made to be right-handed.* . . . Oh, they would whack me over the knuckles when I used my left, those nuns, and maybe, just maybe that is why I hated school so much."

And all his life, he said, his right hand has been a kind of violent weapon. He has smashed it through glass, into concrete, against other people.

"But look at my *left* hand," he said, holding it high. "Not a single scar on it. Long and smooth as a lily . . ."

He paused, then said, "You know, I can write absolutely backwards, mirror writing. . . . Look . . ."

He pulled out his airplane ticket and, with a ballpoint pen, wrote out his name

He laughed. Then, standing and brushing the dirt from his green jacket and trousers, he staggered down the mountain toward the car, and began to leave behind the eerie quiet of the lake, the running trees, and the island of those wizened white nuns.

Looking for Hemingway

I remember very well the impression I had of Hemingway that first afternoon. He was an extraordinarily good-looking young man, twenty-three years old. It was not long after that that everybody was twenty-six. It became the period of being twenty-six. During the next two or three years all the young men were twenty-six years old. It was the right age apparently for that time and place.

GERTRUDE STEIN

Early in the fifties another young generation of American expatriates in Paris became twenty-six years old, but they were not Sad Young Men, nor were they Lost; they were the witty, irreverent sons of a conquering nation and, though they came mostly from wealthy parents and had been graduated from Harvard or Yale, they seemed endlessly delighted in posing as paupers and dodging the bill collectors, possibly because it seemed challenging and distinguished them from American tourists, whom they despised, and also because it was another way of having fun with the French, who despised *them*. Nevertheless, they lived in happy squalor on the Left Bank for two or three years amid the whores, jazz musicians,

103

and pederast poets, and became involved with people both tragic and mad, including a passionate Spanish painter who one day cut open a vein in his leg and finished his final portrait with his own blood.

In July they drove down to Pamplona to run from the bulls, and when they returned they played tennis with Irwin Shaw at Saint-Cloud on a magnificent court overlooking Paris—and, when they tossed up the ball to serve, *there*, sprawled before them, was the whole city: the Eiffel Tower, Sacré-Coeur, the Opéra, the spires of Notre Dame in the distance. Irwin Shaw was amused by them. He called them "The Tall Young Men."

The tallest of them, at six feet four inches, was George Ames Plimpton, a quick, graceful tennis player with long, skinny limbs, a small head, bright blue eyes and a delicate, fine-tipped nose. He had come to Paris in 1952, at the age of twenty-six, because several other tall young Americans— and some short wild ones—were publishing a literary quarterly to be called *The Paris Review,* over the mild protest of one of their staff members, a poet, who wanted it to be called *Druids' Home Companion* and its cover to be birch bark. George Plimpton was made editor-in-chief, and soon he could be seen strolling through the streets of Paris with a long woolen scarf flung around his neck, cutting a figure reminiscent of Toulouse-Lautrec's famous lithograph of Aristide Bruant, that dashing littérateur of the nineteenth century.

Though much of the editing of *The Paris Review* was done at sidewalk cafés by editors awaiting their turns on the pinball machine, the magazine nonetheless became very successful because the editors had talent, money, and taste, and they avoided using such typical little-magazine words as

"Zeitgeist" and "dichotomous," and published no crusty critiques about Melville or Kafka, but instead printed the poetry and fiction of gifted young writers not yet popular. They also started a superb series of interviews with famous authors, who took them to lunch and introduced them to actresses, playwrights, and producers; and everybody invited everybody else to parties, and the parties have not stopped even though a decade has passed, Paris is no longer the scene, and the Tall Young Men have become thirty-six years old.

They now live in New York. And most of the parties are held at George Plimpton's large bachelor apartment on Seventy-second Street overlooking the East River, an apartment that is also the headquarters for what Elaine Tynan calls "The Quality Lit Set," or what Candida Donadio, the agent, calls "The East Side Gang," or what everybody else just calls *"The Paris Review* Crowd."

The parties are usually long and lively, and there are lots of pretty girls and writers and critics, and on the walls there are many photographs of George Plimpton: one shows him fighting small bulls in Spain with Hemingway, another catches him drinking beer with other Tall Young Men at a Paris café, others show him as a lieutenant marching a platoon of troops through Rome, as a tennis player for King's College, as an amateur prizefighter sparring with Archie Moore in Stillman's Gymnasium, an occasion during which the rancid smell of the gymnasium was temporarily replaced by the musk of El Morocco and the cheers of George Plimpton's friends when he scored with a solid jab. But those quickly changed to *"Ohhhhhhhhs"* when Archie Moore retaliated with a punch that broke part of the cartilage in Plimpton's nose, causing it to bleed and causing Miles Davis to ask afterward, "Archie, is that black blood or white blood on your gloves?," to which one of Plimpton's friends replied, "Sir, *that* is blue blood."

Also on the wall is a one-stringed musical instrument made of goatskin that Bedouin tribesmen gave Plimpton prior to his doing a walk-on in *Lawrence of Arabia;* and above his baby grand piano—he plays it well enough to have won a tie-for-third-prize on Amateur Night at the Apollo Theatre in Harlem—is a coconut sent him by a lady swimmer he knows in Palm Beach, and also a photograph of another girl, Vali, the orange-haired Existentialist known to all Left Bank concierges as *la bête,* and also a major-league baseball that Plimpton occasionally hurls full distance across the living room into a short, chunky stuffed chair, using the same windup as when he pitched against big-league hitters while researching his book *Out of My League*, which concerns how it feels to be an amateur among pros—and which, incidentally, is not only a possible key to George Ames Plimpton but to some others on *The Paris Review* as well.

They are obsessed, many of them, by the wish to know how the other half lives. And so they befriend the more interesting of the odd, avoid the downtown dullards on Wall Street, and dip into the world of the junkie, the pederast, the prizefighter, and the adventurer in pursuit of kicks and literature, being influenced perhaps by that glorious generation of ambulance drivers that preceded them to Paris at the age of twenty-six.

In Paris in the early fifties, Irwin Shaw was a sort of pater familias to them because, in the words of Thomas Guinzburg, a Yale man then managing editor of *The Paris Review,* "Shaw was a tough, tennis-playing, hard-drinking writer with a good-looking wife—the closest thing we had to Hemingway." Of course editor-in-chief George Plimpton, then as now, kept the magazine going, kept the group together, and set a style of romanticism that was—and is—infectious.

Arriving in Paris in the spring of 1952 with a wardrobe that included the tails his grandfather had worn in the twenties, and which Plimpton himself had worn in 1951 while attending a ball in London as an escort to the future Queen of England, he moved immediately into a tool shed behind a house owned by Gertrude Stein's nephew. Since the door of the shed was jammed, Plimpton, to enter it, had to hoist himself, his books, and his grandfather's tails through the window. His bed was a long, thin cot flanked by a lawn mower and garden hose, and was covered by an electric blanket that Plimpton could never remember to turn off— so that, when he returned to the shed at night and plopped into the cot, he was usually greeted by the angry howls of several stray cats reluctant to leave the warmth that his forgetfulness had provided.

One lonely night, before returning home, Plimpton took a walk through Montparnasse down the same streets and past the same cafés that Jake Barnes took after leaving Lady Brett in *The Sun Also Rises*. He wanted to see what Hemingway had seen, to feel what Hemingway had felt. Then, the walk over, he went into the nearest bar and ordered a drink.

In 1952 *The Paris Review*'s headquarters was a one-room office at 8 Rue Garancière. It was furnished with a desk, four chairs, a bottle of brandy, and several lively, long-legged Smith and Radcliffe girls who were anxious to get onto the masthead so that they might convince their parents back home of their innocence abroad. But so many young women came and went that Plimpton's business manager, a small, sharp-tongued Harvard wit named John P. C. Train, decided it was ridiculous to try to remember all their names, whereupon he declared that they should henceforth all be called by one name—"Apthecker." And the Apthecker alumnae came to include, at one time or another, Jane Fonda, Joan Dillon Moseley (daughter of Treasury Secretary Dillon), Gail Jones (daughter of Lena Horne), and Louisa Noble (daughter of the Groton football coach), a very industrious but forgetful girl who was endlessly losing manuscripts, letters, dictionaries, and, one day after John P. C. Train received a letter from a librarian complaining that Miss Noble was a year overdue on a book, he wrote back:

Dear Sir:

I take the liberty of writing to you in my own hand because Miss L. Noble took with her the last time she left this office the typewriter on which I was accustomed to compose these messages. Perhaps when she comes into your library you will ask if we might not have this machine.

Subscription blank enclosed.

Yours   faithfully,
J. P. C. Train

Since *The Paris Review*'s one-room office obviously was too small to fulfill the staff's need for mixing business with pleasure, and since there was also a limit to the number of hours they could spend at cafés, everybody would usually gather at 5 P.M. at the apartment of Peter and Patsy Matthiessen on 14 Rue Perceval, where by that time a party was sure to be in progress.

Peter Matthiessen, then fiction editor of *The Paris Review,* was a tall, thin Yale graduate who as a youngster had attended St. Bernard's School in New York with George Plimp-

ton, and who now was working on his first novel, *Race Rock*.
Patsy was a small lovely, vivacious blonde with pale blue
eyes and a marvelous figure, and all the boys of twenty-six
were in love with her. She was the daughter of the late Richard
Southgate, one-time Chief of Protocol for the State Department, and Patsy had gone to the right lawn parties, had
chauffeurs and governesses and, in her junior year at Smith,
in 1948, had come to Paris and met Peter. Three years later,
married, they returned to Paris and acquired for $21 a month
this apartment in Montparnasse that had been left vacant
when Peter's old girl friend had gone off to Venezuela.

The apartment had high ceilings, a terrace and lots of sun.
On one wall was a Foujita painting of a gigantic head of a
cat. The other wall was all glass, and there were large trees
against the glass and wild growth crawling up it, and visitors
to this apartment often felt that they were in a monstrous
fishbowl, particularly by 6 P.M., when the room was floating
with Dutch gin and absinthe and the cat's head seemed
bigger, and a few junkies would wander in, nod, and settle
softly, soundlessly in the corner.

This apartment, in the fifties, was as much a meeting place
for the young American literati as was Gertrude Stein's apartment in the twenties, and it also caught the atmosphere that
would, in the sixties, prevail at George Plimpton's apartment
in New York.

William Styron, often at the Matthiessens', describes their
apartment in his novel *Set This House on Fire,* and other
novelists there were John Phillips Marquand and Terry
Southern, and sometimes James Baldwin, and nearly always
Harold L. Humes, a chunky, indefatigable, impulsive young
man with a beard, beret and a silver-handled umbrella. After
being dismissed from M.I.T. for taking a Radcliffe girl

sailing several hours beyond her bedtime, and after spending
an unhappy tour with the Navy making mayonnaise in Bain-
bridge, Maryland, Harold Humes burst onto the Paris scene
in full rebellion.

He became a chess hustler in cafés, earning several hundred francs a night. It was in the cafés that he met Peter
Matthiessen, and they both talked of starting a little magazine
that would be *The Paris Review*. Before coming to Paris,
Humes had never worked on a magazine, but had grown
fond of a little magazine called *Zero*, edited by a small Greek
named Themistocles Hoetes, whom everybody called "Them."
Impressed by what Them had done with *Zero*, Humes purchased for $600 a magazine called *The Paris News Post*,
which John Ciardi later called the "best fourth-rate imitation
of *The New Yorker* I have ever seen," and to which Matthiessen felt condescendingly superior, and so Humes sold it
for $600 to a very nervous English girl, under whom it col-
lapsed one issue later. Then Humes and Matthiessen and
others began a long series of talks on what policy, if any,
they would follow should *The Paris Review* ever get beyond
the talking and drinking stages.

When the magazine was finally organized, and when
George Plimpton was selected as its editor instead of Humes,
Humes was disappointed. He refused to leave the cafés to sell
advertising or negotiate with French printers. And in the sum-
mer of 1952 he did not hestitate to leave Paris with William
Styron, accepting an invitation from a French actress,
Madame Nénot, to go down to Cap Myrt, near Saint-
Tropez, and visit her fifty-room villa that had been designed
by her father, a leading architect. The villa had been oc-
cupied by the Germans early in the war. And so when

Styron and Humes arrived they found holes in its walls, through which they could look out to the sea, and the grass was so high and the trees so thick with grapes that Humes's little Volkswagen became tangled in the grass.

So they went on foot toward the villa, but suddenly stopped when they saw, rushing past them, a young, half-naked girl, very brown from the sun, wearing only handkerchiefs tied bikini-style, her mouth spilling with grapes. Screaming behind her was a lecherous-looking old French farmer whose grape arbor she obviously had raided.

"*Styron,*" Humes cried, gleefully, "*we have arrived!*"

"Yes," he said, "we are *here!*"

More nymphets came out of the trees in bikinis later, carrying grapes and also half cantaloupes the size of cartwheels, and they offered some to Styron and Humes. The next day they all went swimming and fishing and, in the evening, they sat in the bombed-out villa, a breathtaking site of beauty and destruction, drinking wine with the young girls, who seemed to belong only to the beach. It was an electric summer, with the nymphets batting around like moths against the screen. Styron remembers it as a scene out of Ovid, Humes as the high point of his career as an epicurean and scholar.

George Plimpton remembers that summer not romantically, but as it was—a long, hot summer of frustration with French printers and advertisers; and the other *Review* staff members, particularly John P. C. Train, were so annoyed at Humes's departure that they decided they would drop his name from the top of the masthead, where he belonged as one of the founders, down to near the bottom under "advertising and circulation."

When the first issue of *The Paris Review* came out, in the

spring of 1953, Humes was in the United States. But he had heard what they had done to him and, infuriated, he now planned his revenge. When the ship arrived at the Hudson River pier with the thousands of *Paris Reviews* that would be distributed throughout the United States, Harold Humes, wearing his beret and swearing, *"Le Paris Review c'est moi!"* was at the dock waiting for them; soon he had ripped the cartons open and, with a rubber stamp bearing his name in letters larger than any on the masthead, he began to pound his name in red over the masthead of each issue, a feat that took several hours to accomplish and which left him, in the end, totally exhausted.

"But . . . but . . . how *could* you have *done* such a thing?" George Plimpton asked when he next saw Humes.

Humes was now sad, almost tearful; but, with a final flash of vengeance, he said, "I am damned well not going to get shoved around!"

Rages of this sort were to become quite common at *The Paris Review,* but despite them *The Paris Review* did very well, publishing fine stories by such younger writers as Philip Roth, Mac Hyman, Pati Hill, Evan Connell, Jr., and Hughes Rudd, and, of course, distinguishing itself most of all by its "Art of Fiction" interviews with famous authors, particularly the one with William Faulkner by Jean Stein vanden Heuvel and the one with Ernest Hemingway by Plimpton, which began in a Madrid café with Hemingway asking Plimpton, "You go to the races?"

"Yes, occasionally."

"Then you read *The Racing Form,"* Hemingway said. "There you have the true Art of Fiction."

But, as much as anything else, *The Paris Review* survived because it had money. And its staff members had fun because they knew that, should they ever land in jail, their friends or families would always bail them out. They would never have to share with James Baldwin the experience of spending eight days and nights in a dirty French cell on the erroneous charge of having stolen a bed sheet from a hotel-keeper, all of which led Baldwin to conclude that, while the wretched round of hotel rooms, bad food, humiliating concierges, and unpaid bills may have been the "Great Adventure" for the Tall Young Men, it was not for him because, he said, "there was a real question in my mind as to which would end soonest, the Great Adventure or me."

The comparative opulence of *The Paris Review,* of course, made it the envy of the other little magazines, particularly the staff members of a quarterly called *Merlin,* some of whose editors charged the *Review* people with dilettantism, resented their pranks, resented that the *Review* would continue to be published while *Merlin,* which had also discovered and printed new talent, would soon fold.

In those days *Merlin's* editor was Alexander Trocchi, born in Glasgow of a Scotch mother and Italian father, a very exciting, tall and conspicuous literary figure with a craggy, satanic face, faun's ears, a talent for writing, and a powerful presence that enabled him to walk into any room and take charge. He would soon become a friend of George Plimpton, John Phillips Marquand, and the other *Review* people, and years later he would come to New York to live on a barge, and still later in the back room of *The Paris Review's* Manhattan office, but eventually he would be arrested on narcotics charges, would jump bail, and would leave the United States carrying two Brooks Brothers suits which he had borrowed from George Plimpton. But he would also leave behind a good novel about drug addiction, *Cain's Book,* with its

memorable line: "Heroin is habit-forming . . . habit-forming
. . . rabbit-forming . . . Babbitt-forming."

Alexander Trocchi's staff at *Merlin* in those days was made
up largely of humorless young men in true rebellion, which
The Paris Review staff was not; the *Merlin* crowd also read
the leftist monthly *Les Temps Modernes,* and were concerned
with the importance of being *engagé.* Their editors included
Richard Seaver, who was reared in the Pennsylvania coal-
mine district and in whose dark, humid Paris garage *Merlin*
held its staff meetings, and also Austryn Wainhouse, a dis-
enchanted Exeter-Harvard man who wrote a strong, esoteric
novel, *Hedyphagetica,* and who, after several years in France,
is now living in Martha's Vineyard building furniture according to the methods of the eighteenth century.

While the entire *Merlin* staff was poor, none was so poor
as a poet named Christopher, about whom it was said that
once, when playing a pinball machine in a café, he noticed
a ragged old peasant lady staring at a five-franc piece lying
on the floor near the machine, but before she could pick it
up Christopher's foot quickly reached out and stomped on it.
He kept his foot there while the old lady screamed and while
he continued, rather jerkily, to hold both hands to the machine trying to keep the ball bouncing—and *did,* until the
owner of the café grabbed him and escorted him out.

Some time later, when Christopher's girl friend left him, he
came under the influence of a wild Svengali character then
living in Paris, a pale, waxen-faced painter who was a disciple
of Nietzsche and his dictum "Die at the right time," and who,
looking for kicks, actually encouraged Christopher to commit
suicide—which Christopher, in his depressed state, said he
would do.

Austryn Wainhouse, who had suspected that suicide was
very much on Christopher's mind, had spent the following week

sitting outside of Christopher's hotel each night watching his window, but one afternoon when Christopher was late for a luncheon date with Wainhouse, the latter rushed to the poet's hotel and there, on the bed, was the painter.

"Where's Chris?" Wainhouse demanded.

"I am not going to tell you," the painter said. "You can beat me if you wish; you're bigger and stronger than I, and . . ."

"I *don't* want to beat you," Wainhouse shouted. It then occurred to him how ridiculous was the painter's remark since he (Wainhouse) was actually much smaller and hardly stronger than the painter. "Look," he said, finally, "don't you leave here," and then he ran quickly to a café where he knew he would find Trocchi.

Trocchi got the painter to talk and admit that Christopher had left that morning for Perpignan, near the Spanish border twelve hours south of Paris, where he planned to commit suicide in much the same way as the character in the Samuel Beckett story in *Merlin* entitled "The End"—he would hire a boat and row out to sea, further and further, and then pull up the plugs and slowly sink.

Trocchi, borrowing thirty thousand francs from Wainhouse, hopped on the next train for Perpignan, five hours behind Christopher. It was dark when he arrived, but early the next morning he began his search.

Christopher, meanwhile, had tried to rent a boat, but did not have enough money. He also carried with him, along with some letters from his former girl friend, a tin of poison, but he did not have an opener, nor were there rocks on the beach, and so he wandered about, frustrated and frantic, until he finally came upon a refreshment stand where he hoped to borrow an opener.

It was then that the tall figure of Trocchi spotted him and

placed a hand on Christopher's shoulder. Christopher looked up.

"Alex," Christopher said, casually handing him the tin of poison, "will you open this for me?"

Trocchi put the tin in his pocket.

"Alex," Christopher then said, "what are *you* doing here?"

"Oh," Trocchi said lightly, "I've come down to embarrass you."

Christopher broke down in tears, and Trocchi helped him off the beach, and then they rode, almost in total silence, back to Paris on the train.

Immediately George Plimpton and several others on *The Paris Review* who were very fond of Christopher, and proud of Trocchi, raised enough money to put Christopher on a kind of monthly allowance. Later Christopher returned to London and published books of poetry, and his plays were performed at the Royal Court Theatre in London. Still later he began to write songs for The Establishment, London's satirical night-club act.

After the suicide episode, which, according to George Plimpton, sent at least a half-dozen young novelists to their typewriters trying to build a book around it, life in Paris at the *Review* was once more happy and ribald—but, a year later with the *Review* still doing well, Paris slowly seemed to pall. Paris was, as Gertrude Stein suggested, the right place for twenty-six, but now most of them were thirty years old. And so they returned to New York—but not in the melancholy mood of Malcolm Cowley's exiles of the twenties, who were forced home during the early currents of the crash, but rather with the attitude that the party would now shift to the other side of the Atlantic. Soon New York was aware of their presence, particularly the presence of Harold L. Humes.

After taking over a large apartment on upper Broadway

with his wife, his daughters, and his unclipped wirehaired terrier, and installing seven telephones and a large paper cutter that has the cracking eighteenth-century sound of a guillotine, Humes lashed out with a series of ideas and tall deeds: he hit on a theory of cosmology that would jolt Descartes, finished a second novel, played piano in a Harlem jazz club, began to shoot a movie called *Don Peyote,* a kind of Greenwich Village version of Don Quixote starring an unknown from Kansas City named Ojo de Vidrio, whose girl friend eventually grabbed the film and ran off with it. Humes also invented a paper house, an *actual paper house* that is waterproof, fireproof, and large enough for people to live in; he set up a full-sized model on the Long Island estate of George Plimpton's family, and Humes's corporation, which included some backers from *The Paris Review* crowd, insured Humes's brain for $1,000,000.

During the Democratic National Convention in 1960, Humes led a phalanx of screaming Stevensonians onto the scene after employing the gate-crashing techniques of the ancient armies of Athens. When back in New York he called for an investigation of the New York police force, whereupon the police commissioner called for an investigation of *Humes*—and discovered fourteen unpaid traffic tickets. Humes went to jail just long enough to be discovered by the Commissioner of Corrections, Anna Kross, who upon recognizing him behind bars said, "Why, Mr. Humes, what are *you* doing in *there?*," to which he responded with Thoreau's line to Emerson, "Why, Miss Kross, what are *you* doing out *there?*"

And at the same time, on East Seventy-second Street, the Plimpton parties continue—often being planned only a few hours before they begin. George Plimpton will pick up the phone and call a few people. They, in turn, will call others. Soon there is the thunder of feet ascending the Plimpton staircase. The inspiration for the party may have been that Plimpton won a court-tennis match earlier that day at the Racquet and Tennis Club, or that one member of *The Paris Review* crowd has a book coming out (in which case the publisher is invited to share the expenses), or that a member has just returned to Manhattan from a trip—a trip that might have carried John P. C. Train, a financial speculator, to Africa, or Peter Matthiessen to New Guinea to live with Stone Age tribesmen, or Harold Humes to the Bronx to fight in court over a parking ticket.

And, in giving so many parties, in giving out keys to his apartment, in keeping the names of old friends on *The Paris Review* masthead long after they have ceased to work for it, George Ames Plimpton has managed to keep the crowd together all these years, and has also created around himself a rather romantic world, a free, frolicsome world within which he, and they, may briefly escape the inevitability of being thirty-six.

It exudes charm, talent, beauty, adventure. It is the envy of the uninvited, particularly of some child-bearing Aptheckers in the suburbs who often ask, "When is that group going to settle down?" Some in the group, like George Plimpton, have remained bachelors. Others have married women who like parties—or have been divorced. Still others have an understanding that, if the wife is too tired for a party, the husband goes alone. It is largely a man's world, all of them bound by their memories of Paris and the Great Adventure they shared, and it has very few exiles, although it has had some—one being the beautiful blonde who was very much on everyone's mind in Paris ten years ago, Patsy Matthiessen.

Patsy and Peter are divorced. She is now married to Michael Goldberg, an abstract painter, lives on West Eleventh Street, and moves in the little world of downtown intellectuals and painters. Recently she spent several days in a hospital after being bitten by the dog of the widow of Jackson Pollock. In her apartment she has a cardboard box full of snapshots of *The Paris Review* crowd of the fifties. But she remembers those days with some bitterness.

"The whole life seemed after a while to be utterly meaningless," she said. "And there was something very *manqué* about them—this going to West Africa, and getting thrown in jail, and getting in the ring with Archie Moore. . . . And *I* was a Stepin Fetchit in that crowd, getting them tea at four, and sandwiches at ten. . . ."

A few blocks away, in a small, dark apartment, another exile, James Baldwin, said, "It didn't take long before I really was no longer a part of them. They were more interested in kicks and hashish cigarettes than I was. I had already done that in the Village when I was eighteen or seventeen. It was a little boring by then.

"They also used to go to Montparnasse, where all the painters and writers went, and where I hardly went. And they used to go there and hang around at the cafés for hours and hours looking for Hemingway. They didn't seem to realize," he said, "that Hemingway was long gone."

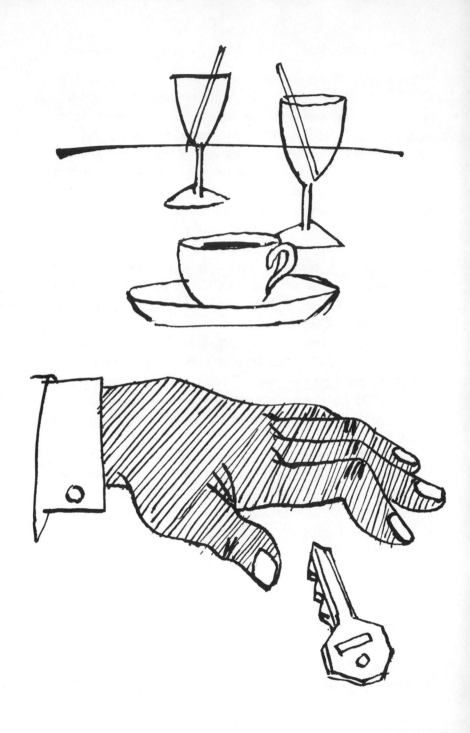

Making the Rounds
with Joe Louis

"Hi, sweetheart!" Joe Louis called to his wife, spotting her waiting for him at the Los Angeles airport.

She smiled, walked toward him, and was about to stretch up on her toes and kiss him—but suddenly stopped.

"Joe," she snapped, "where's your tie?"

"Aw, sweetie," Joe Louis said, shrugging, "I stayed out all night in New York and didn't have time this morning. . . ."

"All *night!"* she cut in. "When you're out here with me all you do is sleep, sleep, sleep."

"Sweetie," Joe Louis said with a tired grin, "I'm an ole man."

"Yes," she agreed, "but when you go to New York you try to be young again."

They walked slowly through the airport lobby toward their car, being followed by a redcap with Joe Louis's luggage. Mrs. Louis, the third wife of the fifty-year-old former fighter, always meets him at the airport when he is returning from a business trip to New York, where he is vice-president of a Negro public-relations firm. She is an alert, pleasingly plump woman in her forties who is a very successful trial lawyer in Los Angeles. She had never known a prizefighter before she met Joe Louis. Previously, she'd been married to a fellow lawyer, a Phi Beta Kappa—a man she described as being "exposed to *books,* not to life." After her divorce, she vowed she wanted a man "exposed to *life,* not books."

She met Joe Louis in 1957 through an introduction from a lady friend on the Coast, and, two years later, to the surprise of her courtroom associates, she married him.

"How in the hell did *you* meet Joe Louis?" they kept asking, to which she replied, "How in the hell did *Joe Louis* meet me?"

Arriving at the car, Joe Louis tipped the redcap and opened the door for his wife. Then he drove past palm trees and quiet neighborhoods for a few miles, and finally turned into a long driveway that flanks an impressive ten-room Spanish-style house worth $75,000. Mrs. Louis bought it a few years ago and filled it with Louis XV furniture—and eight television sets. Joe Louis is a television addict, she explained to her friends, adding that he even has a television set above the bathtub in his bathroom; the set is placed at such an angle that Joe, when taking a shower across the room, can peek over the shower curtain and see a reflection of the TV screen through a strategically placed mirror.

"Television and golf," Mrs. Louis said, helping to carry her husband's things out of the car and into the house, "that's Joe Louis today." She said this unruefully and, later kissing her husband on the cheek, she seemed a lot less formal than she had at the Los Angeles airport. After hanging his coat in the closet, she quickly put on a kettle for tea.

"Cookies, honey?" she asked.

"Nah," Joe Louis said, sitting slope-shouldered at the breakfast table, his eyelids drooping from the lack of sleep in New York.

Soon Mrs. Louis was upstairs, turning down the covers of their gigantic bed, and five minutes later Joe Louis had plunged upon it and was fast asleep. When Mrs. Louis returned downstairs to the kitchen, she was smiling.

"In court, I'm a lawyer," she said, "but when I'm home, I'm *all* woman."

Her voice was husky, suggestive.

"I treat a man *right,* I treat a man like a *king*—if he treats *me* right," she added, pouring herself a glass of milk. "Each morning I bring Joe breakfast in bed. Then I turn on Channel 4 so he can watch the Today Show. Then I go down and get him the Los Angeles *Times.* Then I leave the house for court.

"By 11 A.M.," she continued, "it's time for him to tee off at the Hillcrest Country Club and, if he plays eighteen holes, he should be finished by three o'clock, and will probably drive over to the Fox Hills Country Club for eighteen more. But, if he isn't hitting the ball right, he'll stop after eighteen and go buy a bucket of balls and hit 'em for hours. He don't buy *regular* balls—no, not Joe Louis!—he buys the *Select* balls, the *best,* which cost $1.25 a bucket. And he'll hit, if he's real mad, two, or three, or four bucketfuls, $5 worth. And some nights he comes home, all excited, and says, 'Well, sweetheart, I *finally* got it today! After all these years playing golf, I just realized what I been doing wrong.' But," she said, "a day later he may come home, all mad from throwing clubs, and say, 'I'm never gonna play again!' I'll say, 'But, honey, you told me yesterday you *had* it!' He'll say, 'I *had* it, but I didn't *keep* it!'

"The next morning it might be raining, and I'll say, 'Sweetheart, you gonna play golf today? It's raining.' And he'll say, 'It rains on the course, but it don't rain on the players.' And off to the golf course he goes."

Joe Louis's present wife, Martha, is as different from his first two wives as he is from Martha's Phi Beta Kappa husband. Joe Louis's first wife, Marva, a sleek Chicago stenographer whom he married in 1935 and remarried in 1946, belonged to his lush years, to the years when he blew most of his $5,000,000 boxing fortune on trinkets, jewels, furs, trips abroad, gambling on golf matches, poor investments, lavish tips, and clothes.

Joe Louis's second wife, Rose Morgan, the cosmetics and beauty expert to whom he was married from 1955 to 1958, is a stunning, curvesome woman dedicated to her prosperous business in Harlem, and she refused to stay up all night with him. "I tried to make him settle down," Rose Morgan said. "I told him he couldn't sleep all day and stay out all night any more. He asked me why, and I told him I'd worry and wouldn't be able to sleep. So he said he'd wait till I fell asleep before going out. Well, I stayed up till 4 A.M.—and then *he* fell asleep."

Joe Louis's third wife, Martha, while having none of the obvious sex appeal of the first two, has succeeded where they failed because she is wiser than they, and because Joe Louis was also ripe for taming when he fell in love with her. It does not matter to her that she got Joe Louis in his declining years —at a time when he weighs 240 pounds, is going bald, is somewhat less than prosperous, and no longer possesses the quick reflexes either to hit or pick up checks.

"There's a soul about this man, a quietness that I love," Martha said, adding that her love has been returned. He even goes to church with her, and often appears in court to watch her handle cases, she said. He still goes to night clubs occasionally to hear some of the many musicians and singers he lists among his friends, she said, and she is aware of the number of women who still find Joe Louis sexually appealing, and would consider a night in bed with him time well spent. "But if those sort of women like living on the side streets of a man's life," Martha said, "I wish them well. Yet *I* am his wife, and when I come on the scene they got to get the hell out."

Martha is aware, too, that Joe Louis still is friendly with his two former wives. When he is in Chicago, he often visits Marva (the mother of his two children) and sometimes goes over for dinner. When in New York, he does the same thing with Rose Morgan.

"Joe Louis never really cuts off a woman," Martha observed. "He just adds another to his list."

Joe Louis had told me all about this earlier in the day on the plane coming into Los Angeles from New York, where I'd spent some time following him around Manhattan watching him function as a public-relations executive.

"You know," Joe Louis had said back in New York, "I been married to three of the finest women in the world. My only mistake in life was getting divorced."

"Why did you then?" I asked.

"Oh," he said, "in those days I was married to Marva and Rose I wanted to be free, sometimes just wanted to be alone. I was crazy. I'd go out of the house and stay weeks without coming home. Or maybe I'd stay home in bed for days watching television."

Just as he blames himself for the failure of his first two marriages, so does he accept the blame for all of his other difficulties, such as his inability to hold on to his money, and his negligence in paying taxes. During his visit to New York, some old boxing friends on Eighth Avenue were saying, "Joe, if only you were fighting today, you'd be making twice what you did in the old days, with the money fighters now get from closed-circuit television and all." But Joe Louis shook his head and said, "I ain't sorry I fought when I did. In my time, I made $5,000,000, wound up broke, and owe the Government $1,000,000 in taxes. If I was fighting today, I'd earn $10,000,000, would *still* wind up broke, and would owe the Government *$2,000,000* in taxes."

Though his tax difficulties have eradicated all his assets—including two trust funds he'd set up for his children—Joe Louis is still a man of great pride. He refused the money that hundreds of citizens sent him to help with the Government debt, although he still owes the Government thousands, and could have used the cash. Last year he earned less than $10,000, most of it from personal appearances and endorsements; the last big money he made was the $100,000-a-year guarantee he got in 1956 for wrestling. He won all his matches—except those in which he was disqualified for using his fists—but his career ended not long afterward when the three-hundred-pound cowboy Rocky Lee accidentally stepped on Louis's chest one night, cracking one of his ribs and damaging his heart muscles.

So today Joe Louis's only business interests are with the Louis-Rowe public-relations firm, on West Fifty-seventh Street in Manhattan; his partner, Billy Rowe, is a fast-talking, endlessly articulate Negro who dresses like a Broadway dude, resembles Nat King Cole, and dominates most conversations, although Louis gets in a good line now and then. Billy Rowe, who lives in a fourteen-room house (with four television sets) in the suburbs of New Rochelle, New York, arrives at the office a full hour ahead of Louis, and has the day's—and some of the week's—appointments all lined up by the time Joe Louis strolls in, usually around 11 A.M., with a big wink for the girl at the switchboard.

"Hey, Dad," Billy Rowe greets Louis, "we got an appointment with the mayor on the 13th. We'd had it before, but he's fighting with the governor."

Joe Louis nodded, then yawned, then suddenly became wide-eyed when he noticed walking toward him a voluptuous Harlem night-club singer, a client; without saying a word, the singer swished right up to Joe Louis, wiggled her hips in front of him, and then pressed her large breasts against his hound's-tooth sports jacket.

"You get any closer," Joe Louis said to her, "I gonna have to marry you."

The singer swooned, and slithered away.

"Hey, Dad," Rowe said, looking up from his desk, "you gonna eat lunch at Lindy's?"

"Yeah."

"Who's picking up the check?"

"Yonkers Raceway."

"In that case," Billy Rowe said, "I'll join you."

An hour later, headed for Lindy's, Rowe and Louis left the office and rode down in an elevator crowded with people who grinned or winced as they recognized Joe Louis.

"Hi, champ," they said. "Hello, Joe."

"Sure wouldn't want to start a fight in this car," the elevator man said, grinning.

"No," Joe Louis said, "not enough room for me to run."

"Joe," a man said, shaking Louis's hand, "you sure look in good shape."

"Only in shape for a steak," Louis said.

"Joe," another man said, "seems like only yesterday I seen you fight Billy Conn. Time sure flies."

"Yeah," Louis said, "it do, don't it?"

And on and on it went, as Louis and Billy Rowe walked down Broadway: cab drivers waved at him, bus drivers honked at him, and dozens of men stopped him and recalled how they'd once traveled a hundred thirty miles to get to one of his fights, and how they'd put their heads down to light a cigarette in the first round, then before they could look up Joe Louis had flattened his opponent and they'd missed everything; or how they'd had guests at the house that night to hear the fight, and while they were struggling in the kitchen to get the ice out somebody in the living room yelled, "It's all over! Louis knocked 'im out with the first punch."

It was astonishing, most of all to Joe Louis, that they had remembered him so—especially since he has not had a fight since his unwise comeback in 1951, when Rocky Marciano knocked him out. Two years before that Joe Louis had retired undefeated, having defended his title twenty-five times, more than any other champion.

In Lindy's restaurant, the waiters, fussing over Joe Louis, led him and Rowe to a table occupied by an official from Yonkers Raceway. Before the lunch was half over, Joe Louis was making a pitch for the track's account, saying that a good public-relations campaign by Louis-Rowe would get more Negroes to the track than ever before. The official said he would present their proposal to the board of directors and would let Louis and Rowe know the result.

"Joe, we better get moving," Billy Rowe said, looking at his watch. "We gotta see Joe Glaser. That Joe Glaser's got so much money that the bank charges him storage," Rowe said, laughing at his joke, and added, "Joe, tell that to Glaser when you see him."

Five minutes later, Louis and Rowe were escorted by Glaser's assistants into the new, plush quarters of Mr. Glaser, the talent-booking man, who pounded Joe Louis on the back and said, loud enough for his assistants and secretaries in the other room to hear, "Joe Louis is one of the finest men in the world!"

And Billy Rowe said, because he could not resist, "Joe Glaser's got so much money that the bank charges him storage."

Everybody laughed, except Joe Louis, who glanced sideways at Billy Rowe.

After leaving Glaser's, Louis and Rowe had appointments

at the Investors Planning Corporation of America, where they submitted proposals for selling more mutual funds to Negroes; then visited the Cobleigh and Gordon, Inc., agency, where they discussed a Negro newsletter that Rowe and Louis wish to produce; then dropped into Toots Shor's, and finally went to dinner at La Fonda del Sol, where Rowe had arranged for a couple of Harlem night-club starlets to join them.

"Oh, Joe," one of the girls said, as a Spanish guitar strummed behind her, "when you used to fight, I was a young girl, and in our house we all gathered around the radio— and I wasn't allowed to talk."

Joe Louis winked.

"Joe," another said, "while I'm sitting so close, how's about autographing this menu—for my son?"

Joe Louis grinned, and playfully pulled from his pocket his Park Sheraton Hotel key, dangled it in the air, then slid it across the table to her.

"You don't want to let your son down, do you?" Joe Louis asked.

Everybody laughed, but she did not know whether or not Joe was kidding.

"If I do," she said primly, "I'm sure he'll understand— when he gets older." She slid the hotel key back. Joe Louis howled, and signed the menu.

After dinner, Joe Louis and the rest planned to go night-clubbing in Harlem, but I had an appointment to see Louis's second wife, Rose Morgan. She lives in a large, magnificent uptown apartment that overlooks the Polo Grounds and once was occupied by Joe Louis and his first wife, Marva.

Opening the door, Rose Morgan was chic, impeccably groomed, almost exotic, in a Japanese loll suit. Then, after leading the way across a sprawling, soft thick white rug, and settling herself on a big white sofa, Rose Morgan said, "Oh, I don't know what it was about Joe. He just got under your skin." But being married to Joe Louis was not as exciting as being courted by him, Rose Morgan said, shaking her head. "When I'd come home from work, 6:30 P.M. or 7 o'clock, Joe'd be there watching television and eating apples. But," she continued, after a pause, "we're still very good friends. In fact, I just wrote him a letter the other day telling him I found some things of his around and asked if he wanted them."

"Like what?"

"Well, I have the robe Joe Louis wore when he started boxing, and I have his road shoes, and also the film of the first Billy Conn fight. Got it right here in the closet. Would you like to see it?"

"Certainly would," I said.

Just then, however, Rose Morgan's present husband, an attorney, walked in, followed by some friends from Philadelphia. Rose Morgan's husband is a short, portly, manicured man who, after introducing everyone, suggested a round of drinks.

"I'm just showing Joe's fight film," Rose Morgan said.

"Hate to put you through all the trouble," I said.

"Oh, it's *no* trouble," she quickly said. "I haven't seen it in years. I'd *love* to see it again."

"Is it all right with you if we watch it?" I asked her husband.

"Oh yes, yes, it's all right with me," he said, quietly; it was obvious that he was just being polite, and would rather not have to sit through it. Yet there was no way of stopping his wife, for she quickly had the film projector out of the closet and soon the lights were off in the living room, and the Billy Conn–Joe Louis fight was on.

"Joe Louis was definitely the greatest of all time," one of

the men from Philadelphia was saying, sitting on the sofa, clinking the ice cubes in his glass. "There was a time when nothing was more important to colored people than God and Joe Louis."

The menacing, solemn image of Joe Louis, then twenty-two years younger than he is today, moved across the movie screen toward Billy Conn. When Louis clouted Conn, Billy's bones seemed to shake.

"Joe Louis didn't waste no punches," said one of the men from Philadelphia.

Rose Morgan seemed excited at seeing Joe Louis at his top form, and every time a Louis punch would jolt Billy Conn she'd go, *"Mummmmmmmm"* (sock), *"Mummmmm-mmm"* (sock), *"Mummmmmmmmm"* (sock).

Billy Conn was impressive through the middle rounds, but as the screen flashed "Round 13," somebody in the room said, "Here's where Conn's gonna make his mistake; he's gonna try to slug it out with Joe Louis." Rose Morgan's husband, the lawyer, remained silent, sipping his Scotch.

When the Joe Louis combinations began to land, Rose Morgan went *"Mummmmmmmm, mummmmmm,"* and then the pale body of Billy Conn on the screen began to collapse against the canvas. Billy Conn slowly began to rise. The referee counted over him. Conn had one leg up, then two, then was standing—but the referee forced him back. It was too late.

But Rose Morgan's husband in the back of the room disagreed.

"I thought Conn got up in time," he said, "but that referee wouldn't let him go on."

Rose Morgan said nothing—just swallowed the rest of her drink.

TRAVELING

III
FAST-AND CHIC

Journeying Through *Vogueland*

Each weekday morning a group of suave and wrinkle-proof women, who call one another "dear" and "dahling," and can speak in italics and curse in French, move into Manhattan's Graybar Building, elevate to the nineteenth floor, and then slip behind their desks at *Vogue*—a magazine that has long been the supreme symbol of sophistication for every American female who ever dreamed of being frocked by Balenciaga, shod by Roger Vivier, coiffed by Kenneth, or set free to swing from the Arc de Triomphe in maiden-form mink.

Not since Sappho has anybody worked up such a lather over women as have the editors of *Vogue*. With almost every issue they present stunning goddesses who seemingly become more perfect, more devastating with the flip of each page. Sometimes the *Vogue* model is leaping across the page in mocha-colored silk, or piloting a teak-tipped ketch through the lesser Antilles, or standing, Dior-length, in front of the Eiffel Tower as racy Renaults buzz by—but never hit her —as she poses in the middle of the street, one leg kicking, mouth open, teeth agleam, two gendarmes winking in the background, all Paris in love with her and her dinner dress of mousseline de soie.

At other times the *Vogue* model is wearing "never-out-of-season black" on the Queensboro Bridge with a white cat crawling up her back, a cat she presumably leaves home when she later jets down to Puerto Rico to lunch with Casals while being watched from the hills by native women holding naked children—women who smile at her, admire her silk tussah skirt ("Nantucket nipped"), love her as she spikes up the nine-hole course inside the fortress of old El Morro.

While these fashion models in *Vogue* are merely stupendous, the socialites photographed for that magazine are rich, beautiful, indefatigable, vivid, vital, brilliant, witty, serve on more committees than Congressmen, know more about airplanes than Wolfgang Langewiesche, thrive on country air and yet are equally at home in the smart poker parlors of Cannes; they never age, fade, or get dandruff, and are also (in the words of *Vogue*'s battery of sycophantic caption writers) "amusable," "exquisite," "delicate," "fun," and "smashing."

In one *Vogue* issue, for instance, Mrs. Loel Guinness, photographed before she sashayed from Lausanne to Palm Beach, was described as "vivid, vital, amusing." And, in another issue, Mrs. Columbus O'Donnel possessed a "quick, amused sparkle," Queen Sirikit of Thailand was "amusable, exquisite," and the Countess of Dalkeith was "ravishing" and as effulgent as Lady Caroline Somerset—herself a "delicate moonbeam beauty." Mrs. Murray Vanderbilt, last year a "slender brunette with direct, heartbreaker eyes, and a soft, open laugh," this year is a "beauty with a strong sense of purpose"—her purpose being to fly to Paris to have her portrait painted by "jaunty, rakish" Kees Van Dongen on a Tuesday, and then fly back to New York the same night, "investing," as *Vogue* said, "only 23 hours, 45 minutes."

Should there be that extraordinary case when a celebrated woman in *Vogue* is not a "rare beauty"—as, for instance, when she is almost homely—she is then described as "wise" or "filled with wisdom" or reminiscent of heroines in exquisite, vital novels. Madame Helene Rochas "looks rather like the heroine of a novel by Stendhal." And, should *Vogue* make mention of a non-*Vogue* type, such as Ingrid Bergman, who spends little money in the cosmetic industry, she is credited with having a nose which is "rather generous."

The noses of *Vogue* heroines are usually long and thin, as are the noses of many *Vogue* editors—noses they can look down upon their generally shorter, younger, and less-sophisticated Condé Nast relatives on *Glamour* magazine, also located on the nineteenth floor of the Graybar Building. But it is usually quite simple to tell the two staffs apart because the *jeunes filles* at *Glamour*, in addition to possessing a high quota of noses that *Vogue* might dismiss as "eager, retroussé," are also given to wearing shirt dresses, college-girl circle pins, smiling in the elevator, and saying, "Hi." A *Vogue* lady once described the *Glamour* staff as "those peppy, Hi people."

One day a few years ago a wide-eyed, newly-hired *Vogue* secretary went bouncing into an editor's office with a package, and said, "Hi"—at which the editor is supposed to have cringed, and finally snapped, "We don't say *that* around here!"

"Everyone at *Glamour* of course hopes to work her way up to the *Vogue* staff of grim vigilantes," says the writer Eve Marriam, once a fashion copy editor at *Glamour*. "But it rarely happens. *Vogue* has to be careful. The upcomer might use the word *cute* instead of *panche;* she might talk about giving a *party* instead of a *dinner;* or describe a suède coat 'for weekending with the station-wagon set' rather than 'for your country home.' Or talk of going to a jewelry store instead of a *bijouterie*. Most maladroit of all, she might talk in terms of a *best buy* rather than an *investment,* or a *coup.* Or refer to a *ballgown* as—one shudders to think of it—a *formal.*"

One has only to leave the elevator and enter the nineteenth floor to experience a sudden sensation of being *in Vogue.* The floors are black and star-studded, and the spacious outer room is tastefully furnished with a "delicate, amusable" receptionist with a British accent—perchance in keeping with the magazine's policy of spelling many words the British way: "colour," "honour," "jewellery," and "marvellous" (pronounced *MAA*-vellous!).

To the rear of the receptionist is a curved corridor leading to *Vogue*'s editorial offices. The first office, that of the Beauty Editor, smells of pomades and powders, rejuvenators and other "fountains of youth." Beyond this point, and around a second curve, are a half-dozen offices of other editors, and dividing them is the large, noisy Fashion Room. From nine till five the Fashion Room and the offices around it throb with the shrill, exuberant voices of fifty women, the incessant ring of telephones, the blurred image of leggy silhouettes shooting past, their heels clacking with *élan.* In one corner, the Fabrics Editor picks at silk swatches; in another corner, near a window, the Shoe Editor ponders what's next in "smashing" footwear; in still another corner, the Model Procurer flips through a filing cabinet that contains such highly-classified data on models as which will pose for corset ads, which have the best legs, which have clawlike fingers (ideal for modeling gloves), and which have small, pretty hands (ideal for making small, expensive perfume bottles seem larger).

From the nearby offices of an editor named Carol Phillips ("delicate, amusable, pure-profiled beauty") can be heard the well-bred titters and talk of other *Vogue* tastemakers who stand, arms akimbo, toes pointed out, in front of Mrs. Phillips' desk. Inevitably their chatter blends with the dialogue that ricochets through the corridor, making it at times

most difficult for the Baron De Gunzburg, a senior fashion
editor, to concentrate fully on the London *Times* crossword
puzzle that a messenger fetches for him each morning from
the out-of-town newsstand in Times Square. The Baron, who
is called "Nick-kee" by *Vogue* ladies, and who makes his 7's
in the European style—7—is a former dancer with a Rus-
sian ballet and a one-time actor in a German film called *The
Vampire.* (In the film he played a poet who spent two weeks
in a casket before his chance came to murder the Vampire;
nowadays the Baron is rarely without a black tie, and it is
said that once, while entering a Seventh Avenue elevator
without specifying his choice of floors, he was immediately
whisked up to the floor of a tailor who made uniforms for
undertakers.)

Upstairs from the Baron, in one of the few offices occupied
by *Vogue* on the twentieth floor, Feature Editor Allene Talmey, whom Crowninshield once described as a "Soufflé of
Crowbars," bats out her famous column "People Are Talking
About"—a collection of items that she and other *Vogue*
ladies are talking about, and think *everybody* should be talking about. She writes:

PEOPLE ARE TALKING ABOUT . . . the present need for the Greek
    word, *bottologia,* meaning much speaking, or vain repeti-
    tions, as used by St. Matthew (6:7) . . .
PEOPLE ARE TALKING ABOUT . . . the Christening presents given
    to the daughter of the great Austrian conductor, Herbert von
    Karajan . . .
PEOPLE ARE TALKING ABOUT . . . Takraw, a game beautiful to
    watch . . .
PEOPLE ARE TALKING ABOUT . . . Hummingbirds . . .
PEOPLE ARE TALKING ABOUT . . . the Eastern half of the world . . .

While some of *Vogue*'s critics contend that the magazine's
literary policy can be summed up with "When in Doubt, Re-

print Colette," it must be said in *Vogue*'s behalf that it has printed work by some excellent writers, among them Marianne Moore, Jacques Barzun, Rebecca West, and Allene Talmey. And yet one of *Vogue*'s former art directors, the inimitable Dr. Mehemet Femy Agha, once said, "Although Allene is wonderful. I've often told her she's like a piano player in a whorehouse. She may be a very good piano player, but nobody goes there to hear music. Nobody buys *Vogue* to read good literature; they buy it to see the clothes."

Among the first to see the clothes is the Baron De Gunzburg, who, having finished the London *Times* crossword puzzle, is now in the Garment Center on Seventh Avenue reclining in a posh divan in the showroom of the clothier Herbert Sondheim, who is giving *Vogue* magazine a private preview of Sondheim's spring frocks. Sitting next to the Baron is another *Vogue* editor, Mildred Morton ("pure-profiled blonde with slightly bored, raised eyebrow").

"You are the first persons in the entire world to be seeing these," says Mr. Sondheim, a short, rather stout, gravel-voiced man who rubs his hands, smiles from ear to ear.

A moment later a blonde model appears from behind the curtain, prances toward the Baron and Mrs. Morton, and coos, "Number 628."

The Baron writes down the style number in his Hermes leather notebook, and watches her twirl around, and then walk back through the curtain.

"That's pomecia," says Mr. Sondheim.

"Expensive?" asks Mrs. Morton.

"Pomecia cotton is about $2.50 a yard," Mr. Sondheim says.

"Number 648," says a second model, a brunette, who slithers past Mr. Sondheim, dips, then twirls around in front of the Baron De Gunzburg.

"Awfully smart," says the Baron, letting his fingers give the model's pomecia evening dress a professional pinch. "I just *love* the slashed coat."

Mrs. Morton raises her right eyebrow.

"Are you getting away this winter?" the Baron asks Mr. Sondheim.

"Probably," he says. "Palm Beach."

The Baron seems unimpressed.

"Number 624," announces the brunette model, appearing again with a flourish of frock, a dip, a spin.

"Wonderful texture, pomecia," Mr. Sondheim says, quickly getting businesslike again. "Furthermore, it doesn't crease."

"Like the other two better, don't you, Nick-*kee?*" asks Mrs. Morton.

The Baron is silent. The model twirls in front of him again, then stands with her back to him.

"What is your number?" the Baron asks, in a clipped British tone.

"Numba 6 3 9," she shoots back over her shoulder. The Baron writes it down, and then watches the model disappear behind the curtain to the clatter of plastic hangers.

Five minutes later, Mr. Sondheim's collection has been shown, and the Baron gives him the style numbers of the dresses *Vogue* wishes to have photographed and shown exclusively. Mr. Sondheim is delighted to comply, for having clothes appear first in *Vogue*'s editorial pages almost guarantees their successful sale.

It all started back on December 17, 1892, when "quiet, clubby" Arthur Baldwin Turnure (Princeton '76), husband of one of America's first lady golf bugs, founded *Vogue* magazine. By 1895 he had created a sensation by displaying in his magazine the dresses and underwear to be worn by Miss Consuelo Vanderbilt on the occasion of her marriage to the Duke of Marlborough.

In 1909 *Vogue* was purchased by Condé Nast, under whom it flourished as never before, and no other magazine in the fashion field has ever been able to challenge it. *Harper's Bazaar*, which has always been less conservative—"It goes one rhinestone too *far*," a *Vogue* lady explains—does not provide its readers with quite so much of what Mary McCarthy calls "Democratic snobbery."

Some years ago Miss McCarthy, who did a rather extensive study of women's fashion magazines for *The Reporter*, concluded that as one descended through the less chichi magazines—such as *Charm, Glamour, Mademoiselle*—one found more genuine solicitude for the reader and her problems—"the pain of being a B.G. (Business Girl), the envy of superiors, self-consciousness, awkwardness, loneliness, sexual fears, timid friendliness to the Boss, endless evenings with the mirror and the tweezers, desperate Saturday social strivings ('Give a party and ask *everyone* you know'), the struggle to achieve any identity in the dead cubbyhole of office life."

And in another study of female magazines, this one done in *Social Forces* by two sociologists, Bernard Barber of Barnard College and Lyle S. Lobel, then of Harvard, it was stated that while the symbols of prestige in *Vogue* were "sophistication and chic," these same symbols were scorned by the respectable, PTA-types on the *Ladies' Home Journal*, where there "is a distaste for 'high style,' for what is 'daring' or 'unusual.' "

But above *Vogue's* ultra-chic level, according to the sociologists, there looms an even more-envied class of women: the unfashionable "old money" rich.

"At this top-most level, where there is little need to compete for status through consumption," wrote Barber and

Lobel, "women may even maintain a certain independence of current changeful 'fashion.' Their quality clothes can remain roughly the same for several years. . . . Even eccentric, like the old ladies on Beacon Street in Boston."

Describing the *Vogue* level, they continued: "In the social class just below the 'old money' families we find most of the 'high fashion,' Paris-conscious style leaders. Since they are aware of the class above, perhaps trying to gain entrance into it, these women seek to combine opulence with 'quiet elegance.' 'Fashion copy' for this group stresses the *pose* of assured distinction, effortless superiority, and inbred elegance."

Before *Vogue* magazine can display its pose of assured distinction and elegance, of course, it must summon its high-fashion models and have them photographed by fashion photographers, and on this particular afternoon *Vogue*'s colour photography sitting was being held in the penthouse studio of the noted photographer Horst Horst, a marvellous spot overlooking the East River. In the studio, while Horst Horst adjusts his German, Japanese, and Swedish cameras, his Chinese houseboy tacks enormous sheets of balmy sky-blue cardboard to the wall, creating a summery background. In the middle of the floor, in front of a box of flowers, is a plush stool of warm, Hazelmu brown on which the model will sit. In the adjoining dressing room, *Vogue*'s Mrs. Simpson, while awaiting the arrival of the model, Dorothea McGowan, does needlepoint from a Matisse pattern.

"I'd go mad, *mad* without this," Mrs. Simpson says of her needlepoint.

In another corner of the dressing room, *Vogue*'s wardrobe mistresses press a half-dozen Galanos chiffon gowns that the model will wear. Finally, ten minutes later, Dorothea McGowan, a tall, pale girl, lunges in with her hair in curlers. Immediately she removes her coat, unhinges her hair, dashes for the mirror, and quickly begins to stroke her canvaslike facial skin with a Japanese paint brush.

"Which shoes, Mrs. Simpson?" she asks.

"Try the red ones, dear," Mrs. Simpson says, looking up from Matisse.

"Let's go," calls Horst from the other room.

Within a few minutes, after expert facial painting, Dorothea transforms herself from the pale, gangling Brooklyn girl she'd been upon entering the studio into a sophisticated, ageless woman about to pose for her seventh *Vogue* cover. She walks confidently into the studio, stands fifteen feet in front of Horst, stretches her calf muscles, spreads her legs slightly, places hands on hips, and prepares for her love affair with the camera.

Horst Horst, hands caressing his tripod, crouches and is about to shoot when Mrs. Simpson, standing on the sidelines like a duenna, shouts, "Wait." And the trance is momentarily broken as Mrs. Simpson says, "Her nails look terrible."

"Do they?" asks Dorothea, no longer the confident woman, but now again the girl from Brooklyn.

"Yes, do you have your nails with you?"

The model goes into the dressing room to put on her false nails, and then returns in front of the camera. Mrs. Simpson, satisfied now, returns to her needlepoint in the next room, and the Chinese boy places a fan in front of Dorothea, blowing her chiffon dress into her thin, lean body.

Dorothea throws her head back.

"Oh, such a rich feeling when the fan blows," she titters.

"Do something with your leg," Horst says.

She bends it backward, opens her mouth. And Horst's camera goes *click*. Then she leans down against the stool, lips puckered. Horst goes *click*.

"Oh, that's good," Horst says. "Do it again" (click).

Dorothea smiles (click); opens her mouth (click); wider, a big O (click).

"Hat's coming off," she giggles.

"Just smile, don't grin," he says (click). "Make a long neck."

She stretches (click).

"That's my girl," he says (click).

"Yesss," he repeats slowly (click).

And now, without any directions from him, she automatically strikes different poses, each one punctuated with a click; her face now bitchy, now primed for love, now blazy-eyed, now as demure as a Vassar virgin's. And Horst all the while is saying, excitedly behind the camera,

"Yesss" (click), "Yesss" (click), "Yesss" (click).

"What are these little flowers?" Dorothea asks finally, breaking out of the mood.

"Azaleas," Horst says, lighting a cigarette. Dorothea pulls off a large rhinestone ring from her right hand, places it on her left, and then says, "You know, if you take a ring off one finger and put it on another finger, it still feels like you have it on the first finger."

Horst Horst looks at her in mild wonderment. Then Dorothea goes to change her dress. And the Chinese boy, built like a speed swimmer, turns off the fan and quickly changes the background from blue cardboard to pink. When Dorothea returns, Mrs. Simpson is back for another look.

"Dorothea," Mrs. Simpson says, "you have little hairs sticking out in the back of your neck."

"Oh?" Dorothea says, touching her neck.

Dorothea, turning toward the dressing room, notices the pink background, and her face becomes alive with anticipation.

"Oh," she exclaims, "I have pink . . . pink, PINK!"

Social Climbing

on the Slopes

Each Friday afternoon they gather along Park Avenue wearing their Aspen-raced ski parkas (which are mildew-proof, crease-resistant, and allergy-free) and their slim, zippered stretch pants (pickpocket-proof), and wait for the chalet bus that will soon transport them up to a glorious ski weekend at Sugarbush, Vermont—where they might break a leg.

Such grim possibilities, however, do not haunt them.

"If you ski, you're going to break something sooner or later," said Mary Baker, an attractive brunette stoic, casually shrugging her shoulders under her expensive black fur parka. "And besides," she went on, "breaking a leg is no worse than having a baby."

Though she spoke with somewhat limited authority—she has had two babies, but so far she has only broken an arm—her friends standing along the sidewalk quickly agreed. They were all young, happy people of great energy and optimism; their only problem now was that merely three months of ski weather remained, and the chalet bus was five minutes late. But finally somebody yelled, "Here it comes!" and soon the big vehicle, driven by a swinging driver named Johnny McBride, who used to chauffeur Count Basie's band, stopped on Fifty-first Street and, amid the clatter of skis and clinking of bottles, everybody hopped on, knowing everyone else in the bus, or thinking they did.

"We've met somewhere," says the young Wall Street broker to the slinky blonde sitting across the aisle. "Was it at Squaw Valley?"

"No," she says, demurely.

"Kitzbühel?"

"I don't think so."

"Wait!" he exclaims, with a gleam of recognition. "It was at Bunnie's wedding!"

"Oh, *yes!*" she shrieks, and he breaks out a bottle of Scotch and hands her a cup.

The bus, meanwhile, is moving swiftly through the suburbs and exurbs, then dipping down into the narrow, winding roads of smaller towns, and finally climbing into the hills of New England and not stopping until, six hours and 288 miles later, it crosses into Vermont and reaches that frosty joyland—Sugarbush.

Sugarbush, as those who glide through the glossy pages of ski magazines already know, is the most chic snow spa in the eastern portion of the United States. Opening in December, 1958, and quickly being nicknamed "Mascara Mountain" and "El Morocco on the Rocks," it styles itself after the fashionable slopes of Europe; its skiers, without having to risk a single hair blowing out of place, can ride to the summit of the four-thousand-foot mountain within glass-enclosed, wind-proof gondolas, which are globe-shaped, and which look, as they hover over the white trails and trees, like an endless skytrain of varicolored apples on sticks.

It is too late for skiing when the Park Avenue bus arrives Friday night, but by 10 A.M. the next morning the slopes are slippery with sophisticates. There are women in Christian Dior pants and parkas lined with Scottish fleece and rimmed with silver fox. And there are men in Garmisch boots cut from the hides of sheltered Bavarian steers—and flamboyant, quilted parkas flapping with various cardboard tags indicating that either the parkas or the wearers (and possibly both) have skied in such places as Chamonix, St. Moritz, Klosters, or Cortina d'Ampezzo.

The slopes of Sugarbush are superbly conditioned for social climbing. And at the top, though they may number less than one hundred of the twenty-four hundred that ski Sugarbush on a busy day, is Café Society's heralded Jet Set. The Jet Set usually is the last to arrive on the slopes; many of them have their own chalets at Sugarbush and rise late for breakfast, not being subjected, as are guests who live in ski lodges, to the 9 A.M. closing of dining room doors by the ski bums who work in the kitchens and want to clean up fast and get to the snow themselves. So the Jet Set can arrive late, and they also seem casual and calm in slipping on their parkas and Baruffaldi Italian goggles, and when they finally leave the chalets and appear on the slopes they move slowly, confidently toward the gondola. They seem to *know* they'll get a seat.

At lunchtime, the Jet Set does not have to condone the clatter of Sugarbush's large, noisy cafeteria; they retire, instead, to a private little club founded in 1959 by the Cassini brothers, four other rich Americans, and a few rich Greeks—and they named it "Skiclub 10."

The ten soon multiplied to almost ten times the original number, including such personages as Prince Sadruddin Aga Khan and Count Demetrio Guerrini-Maraldi—although the club's building itself has remained small and unostentatious, its entire floor space not seeming much larger than a basketball court.

But seated around this floor, along the dark blue banquettes amid the smoke of Turkish tobacco and music from *La Dolce Vita,* are some of the most slumberously sleek and exquisitely elegant women ever to have schussed through a ski boutique. They do not possess the sweet, college-girl look of most of those in the cafeteria, girls whose confidence comes from a surfeit of attention from college boys. The Skiclub 10 women are older, between twenty-seven and thirty-two and, as F. Scott Fitzgerald once said in another time, they are "nourished on subtler stuff" and "choose apéritifs wisely." There is just the slightest trace of boredom in their manner, just the right amount of challenging coolness. Nearly all of them are excellent skiers, but they ski only when conditions are good; otherwise, they spend the day at Skiclub 10 sipping orange juice mixed with white wine and playing bridge or backgammon with the men.

The men are also very attractive—or, if not attractive, very rich; or, if not rich, very talented; or, if not talented, very useful to the club—or, if not useful, they never get into the club.

Here, with the temperature close to zero, Nan Kempner, a delicate beauty in an ocelot parka, plays cards with Louise Collins, the blonde television actress and widow of Peter Collins, the British racing driver; while at an adjoining table, suffering slightly from a touch of frostbite on the ear, is the musician Skitch Henderson, and across from him is Carlos de Bourbon, brother of Spain's next king, and next to him is John Braganza, pretender to the Portuguese throne, all laughing and having fun—all except Harry Theodoracopulos, the Greek shipping scion, who is not doing anything.

"H-a-r-r-y," calls a throaty redhead from across the room, "br-i-i-dge?"

He shakes his curly head. He is thinking. He is a very serious man of thirty, a big, broad-shouldered bachelor who says, "I do not share in this Anglo-Saxon belief that if you are involved with a girl you should marry." He works hard in his family's business, plays hard at tennis, drives a sports car, and took up skiing a few years ago. Harry learned quickly, but he does not need the prestige of a broken limb, so he holds himself back. "What slows me down is I cannot afford to get hurt," he says. "I have to go to the office. So I try to ski within my limits, even if little kids whiz by me. I check my equipment very carefully, and I do not ski when conditions are hazardous, like today. I exercise every other evening in a gymnasium, and I always try to avoid breaking anything."

Harry Theodoracopulos is a typical male member of the Jet Set. He is not in the moody, restless tradition of the European playboy who cavorts all night and sleeps through most of the afternoon; he, like most other men in the set, takes work very seriously. He plays hard, works hard. He tries to keep ever on the move, jetting here and there, spiking his life whenever possible with lovely women, delectable food, and vivacious companions in fashionable places.

On the trail of the Jet Set is another high-octane crowd of skiers. But they are younger, less continental. While they are attractive and carefully dressed—a number of them came up to Sugarbush on the Park Avenue chartered bus on Friday night—they have not *yet* made it big on Wall Street or in the professions, and they are not *yet* ready to splurge on a private chalet in the mountains. They are, in a sense, still in the turbo-prop class, but they are formidable, up-and-coming types only temporarily traveling tourist-class behind the Jet Set. While they patronize the ski lodges and are forced to rise early before the breakfast room closes, they are always careful to be in the better lodges, such as the Alpen Inn, which is well-equipped and friendly, and which has in the kitchen some ski bums listed in the Social Register.

Also visible on the slopes of Sugarbush, and quite distinguishable from the Turbo-Prop Set and the Jet Set, and those masses who just came to ski, is a frosty faction of rebels that reject everything the Jet Set lives by. This rebel group, composed mostly of college or post-graduate skiers, bunk in run-down ski lodges, often wear blue jeans instead of ski pants, and have been known even to ski at Sugarbush with long red underwear *over* their blue jeans.

It is as if they wish to deface the glamour that prevails along the mountain, wish to see skiing return to the raw, unself-conscious era of thirty years ago—before stretch pants, before the mode of après-ski life. But these purists are fighting impossible odds. The world of high fashion has indisputably conquered the hills of Sugarbush, and the hills around it, and so has the skier who wouldn't think of wearing the same parka two days in a row. Even the ski patrol's medical teams have become fashion conscious. "At almost any other place, when a lady skier breaks a leg, they automatically cut right through the stretch pants to attend the wound," explains one medic. "But here we try to be careful never to cut pants; or, if we must cut, we try to cut along the seam. Sugarbush wishes to keep *all* its skiers looking trim," he says, "even its casualties."

Going Nowhere with Christina

When the doorman in the lobby of the Park Avenue apartment saw Christina Paolozzi, the lovely blonde daughter of Italy's Count Lorenzo Paolozzi, stepping out of the elevator behind her dog and walking toward him, he became very tense. Her dog, a pampered Pomeranian named Lupino, was unleashed, as it always is, and the doorman knew that if he hoped to avoid chasing the animal down the street, while pedestrians laughed and while Christina waited impatiently at the curb yelling, *"Lupino, Lupino!,"* he had better intercept the dog at once.

But, when he reached down to grab Lupino, the dog snapped at him, darted between his legs, raced out the door, and scampered down Park Avenue.

"Lupino, Lupino!" cried Christina Paolozzi, as the doorman, swearing and beginning to sweat, chased down Park Avenue after her pet.

People paused to watch. Automobile traffic stopped. A jam resulted. Horns honked. There was noise, confusion. And Christina Paolozzi had what she'd wanted—attention. She will do anything to get it. She posed in the nude for *Harper's Bazaar*. She throws wild parties, cracks up cars, skis recklessly, is the darling of the Jet Set.

She was among the first of this rich clique of international thrill seekers in recent years to go slumming in Harlem, to twist at the Peppermint Lounge—and, in Palm Beach, she and other "revolutionaries" were busy organizing a force to attack Castro, and might have tried had not the State Department suddenly banned such extravaganzas.

While Christina Paolozzi has many whimsical pursuits, she is neither very dedicated nor talented in any of them. She cannot be classified as an actress, although she has played small parts and was the only performer in *La Dolce Vita* who was not acting. She is not a top model because she refuses to get up in the morning. She is not a painter, although she dabbles at it; not a dancer, although she takes lessons; not a writer, although she has written part of a novel—a largely autobiographical tale of wild scenes on yachts and in villas. She is not even beautiful. While she has a fine Botticelli face with large brown eyes and a thin nose—a nose which was reshaped for her at a cost of $300—she has thick hips and ordinary legs. When she appeared bare-chested in *Harper's Bazaar,* newspaper columnist Inez Robb said it proved that "not diamonds but clothes are a girl's best friend."

If she is neither beautiful, talented, nor dedicated, why is Christina Paolozzi influential? Why do so many people talk *about* her, react *to* her?

If there is any explanation other than the obvious fact that she is an exhibitionist, it is that Christina Paolozzi, somehow, has become a living symbol of the Soft Life of the Sixties, and is even regarded as *symbolic of Western decadence* by the Communist party in Italy. This is what happens, they say, when an individual has too much money, too much time, and no purpose. The Leftist press in Italy rarely misses a chance to show her twisting at a night club, lolling in the sun in a bikini, or getting shoved into somebody's pool.

However, the editors of *Harper's Bazaar* defend her on the grounds that she is chic: she is the first, they say, to seize any new idea in make-up, coiffure, dress, and to turn the idea inspiredly to her own ends, and then, quickly bored, to discard it —"relinquishing a look not before it grows old, *but even before it is news.*"

To New York's Republican Senator, Jacob K. Javits, Christina Paolozzi is "one of the last of the free spirits" in this age of conformity. To Richard Avedon, she is the "divine discontent," and to society columnist Joseph X. Dever, she exudes a kind of "charming lawlessness" that is becoming increasingly rare in America today. "She appeals to those caught in the dull, gray monotony of life," Mr. Dever says, adding that she provides vicarious thrills, a sense of shock, and heightened anticipation over what zany thing she may do next.

Almost from the moment she gets up in the morning, or afternoon, Christina Paolozzi exhibits a restlessness that is mollified only when she gets attention.

"Guess I'm a bitch," she says casually, walking barefoot through her mother's Park Avenue apartment. "I guess it all started when, as a child trying to get attention, I kept getting cut up, beat up, or breaking my neck in slalom races. I broke my hip, leg, arms—all for attention. It was the only way I thought I could get my mother back from Africa, or wherever she happened to be at the time. . . ."

When her parents separated, Christina Paolozzi said, her family lost some of its social position among Italian nobility; but this had little to do with her own rebellion, she said, because she had long ago decided she wanted nothing to do with the quiet life then demanded of Italian debutantes.

"In Rome, when I was growing up, it was *not* very fashionable to be sportive, it was just fashionable to watch," she said. "It was *not* fashionable to be an excellent dancer, but *was* fashionable to be at every ball. It was also fashionable to pass the days in needlepoint, and each day have a masseuse come in —at least *I* did—and to lunch at 2 P.M. at the golf club or polo fields and *watch*.

"Well, I could not accept all this. Besides, Mother had tried for years to be social in Italy. It nearly drove her nuts."

She paused, glanced at her watch.

"Oh," she said, "I'm late. I should be at the model agency."

She called her Pomeranian, *"Lupino, Lupino!"*

The dog, dragging a large, greasy chicken bone across an expensive Chinese rug, ran through the living room. Ten minutes later, after the doorman had chased Lupino halfway around the block, Christina was sitting in a cab, en route to her modeling agency.

"My problems are so ridiculous," she said, petting her dog, the cab moving down Park Avenue. "Too much money. Too many playgrounds. I'm actually tired of being the poor little rich girl, but I guess I just do not want to face life as it is. It would be too boring. And yet," she went on, "I'm very naïve. For instance, when I posed in the nude for *Harper's Bazaar,* well, it never occurred to me that the world would judge me for *that*. But the results were ridiculous. I could not leave the apartment. I got calls from friends saying their breasts were ten times more beautiful than mine, and asked, 'How dare you sit there and show *them?'* I was taken off all the ball committees and charity balls. I was dropped from the Social Register. In Rome, the people who used to come to my pool and swim stopped coming. My only friends that summer were press agents, photographers, and newspapermen. I didn't see one aristocrat all summer!"

She stopped talking, gazed through the cab window toward a tall blonde woman strolling across Fifty-sixth at Park in a leopard-skin coat.

"What a lovely person," Christina said. Then added, "But she doesn't know how to walk."

At Fifty-fifth Street, in front of her modeling agency, Christina got out. Lupino sprinted down the sidewalk.

"Lupino, Lupino!" Christina shouted.

Men turned and smiled at her. Women eyed her coolly.

Finally, when Lupino returned, she picked him up, held him during the elevator ride in the office building, then released him inside the model-agency office so that his barking would announce her presence.

"Hello, Christina," said the receptionist quickly, before returning to her chewing gum.

"Hi, Christina," called a trim, effeminate man, in a tired voice, standing near a filing cabinet.

"I do *not* like the greeting I'm getting today," Christina announced. "I think I shall go out, *and come in again."*

She went out, and came in again.

"Contessa, dah-ling!" cried the trim, effeminate man, rushing to embrace her as she strode through the doorway. The receptionist gave her a big smile, removing her gum.

"That's better," Christina said.

Then she walked toward the office of the agency's president, who wanted her to sign a new contract.

"They need me more than I need them," Christina said. "They like all that publicity I get them."

While the agency president, a bald-headed, nervous man, beamed at her over his desk, Christina Paolozzi read the small print on the reverse side of the contract.

"I *wish* I could read English better," she said.

"You read all right, baby," he said. "Only thing you don't read is the clock."

"That's not true," she protested, lightly. "They all book me a second time, don't they?"

"They do because you're beautiful, not because you're on time," he said, smiling again, waiting anxiously for her to sign the contract.

"Oh, I wish I had good, sharp lawyers," she said, deliberately delaying him, seeming to delight in his uneasiness.

A few moments later, after crossing her legs a few times and doodling along the edge of the contract, she finally signed. He exhaled. He smiled and took her hand. Then she got up, turned and walked into the other room to put on her coat. He said, "Just think, couple years ago that Christina was a kooky kid, but now she's developing into . . . developing into . . ." he groped for the word, but, failing to get it, said finally, ". . . into a *lady"*—and let it go at that.

"What are you telling him?" Christina said, coming back into his office.

"Nice things," said the president.

"Good," she said. "Incidentally," she went on, "I hear you are cutting down on a few models."

"Yes," he said.

"Good," she said.

Then, waving at everybody, she yelled "Ciao," and everybody waved back, smiling, "GOOD-BYE, CHRISTINA! CIAO, CONTESSA!"

Next, because she had a slight, recurring skin rash, Christina hailed a taxicab to take her uptown to her doctor, but when she arrived the nurse told her she would have to wait a few moments.

Christina paced the floor. Lupino nipped at the heels of two other patients in the waiting room.

"Oh, I *hate* waiting," she muttered. "That doctor is paying me back for all the times I've kept *him* waiting."

Ten minutes later, however, she was called in, and the doctor, a portly middle-aged man with horn-rimmed glasses, was very pleasant.

"When did the itch come back, Christina?"

"It was fine for two days in Palm Beach, then it came back."

"Well," he said, studying his chart, "let's review. Could it be Coca-Cola?"

"I *must* drink Coca-Cola," she said. "I *can't* help it. Maybe my rash came back because of the tension of my being back to work at modeling."

"I doubt it," said the doctor.

"I think it could be the tension over Cuba," she said. "This has got me upset, this and my boy friend, Juan José . . ."

"It's probably food," he said.

"You're convinced it's food; *I'm* convinced it isn't!" she said, sharply.

"Look, Christina," he said, patiently, "what do you want us to do?"

"Find out what it is."

"And then, when we do, what?"

"That depends on what it is."

He went back to his chart, and she, kicking up her feet, said, "Doctor, do you know where I can get a nursing home?"

"Why?"

"It's my maid. She's very upset."

"What about?"

"She's upset about the city hospital here. They won't accept my maid's sister as a nut."

"Oh," the doctor said, barely listening.

One hour later, Christina Paolozzi was taking dancing lessons at the June Taylor studio, then she taxied back to her mother's apartment on Park Avenue. But when the cab pulled in at the curb, the doorman rushed forward and told Christina not to come in, that her mother had left instructions that she was barred from the apartment because of the way it had been left after Christina's party of the night before.

Turning in rage, Christina went to her own apartment a few blocks away in the East Fifties. The next day, in the newspapers, there was an item reporting an explosion in Christina Paolozzi's apartment. It said that the beautiful, rich "playgirl" had required medical care for burns.

The Road to Romy

On the movie set she was the star, the little princess, and Otto Preminger put an avuncular arm around her and hugged her, and the studio photographers rushed in, cameras clicking, and pleaded, *"One more,* Romy; *one more,* please."

Romy Schneider posed for a few moments but then, quickly bored, said, "Stop, no more!"—and they stopped.

It was an afternoon in Rome, and Preminger's film was nearly finished, and Romy Schneider was anxious to get back to the hotel.

"But, Romy," cried the publicity man, "you have interviews scheduled for today."

"Not today," she snapped. "Today I am tired. Maybe tomorrow."

And off she went in her Karman-Ghia, leaving the publicity man to explain that she was probably upset because her boy friend, the actor Alain Delon, had not telephoned her this morning from Tokyo. The movie journalists and magazine writers were disgusted, and some asked themselves: *Why do we, who might otherwise be interviewing people of Meaning, pursue these silly movie stars?* . . . forgetting that such stars have more meaning for more people than all the Adlai Stevensons, the Barry Goldwaters, the Margaret Meads, the Sirimavo Bandaranaikes, the Marianne Moores, the Jomo Kenyattas, because the star, alas, bestows glorious hours of escape upon the world, and Miss Schneider, at the age of twenty-four, knew this.

But she had waited a long time before earning the right to be late. She had waited, as a little girl, in hotel suites each night for her mother, a divorced actress, to return from the theatre; she had waited for years to shatter her teenage image as a Teutonic Shirley Temple before getting parts in *The Trial* and *Boccaccio 70, The Cardinal,* and *The Victors;* she had to wait until 1963 before the magazine writers and journalists paid her any attention . . . and so now she was letting *them* wait . . . and they waited in Rome for three days, cursing and chasing her . . . and when they finally caught up with her . . . she was beautiful.

She was a little girl, a very little girl with large green eyes, a sweet smile, and a soft voice that said, "I must go to the eye doctor . . . *you will come with me?"*

Along the way she talked about how her parents' divorce depressed her; about how proud she was of her brother, Wolfgang, a medical student in Switzerland; about her tempestuous relationship with Alain Delon; about how she sometimes is so high-strung that she breaks out all over in an ugly skin rash; and, shaking her head, she said, "Oh, I am so spoiled as a child. I got everything I wanted. But in Germany the newspapers think just so they spell my name right they can write whatever they please. . . ."

"Oh, Romy, don't worry; there are so many finks on newspapers writing about films."

"Finks?" she asked. "What means *fink?"*

"A fink is an idiot, a nudnick."

The word delighted her.

"Fink!" she said. *"FINK!"* she repeated louder, and giggled as she skipped lightly through the street.

Back in her hotel suite, a picture of Delon over her bed, her clothes closets filled by Chanel, her bathroom lined with cosmetic jars, a private drugstore, she poured out two Scotches, kicked off her shoes, and flipped her small phonograph to the theme from *Mondo Cane*—and, lying on the floor in her tight black Bogners and black cashmere sweater, she sipped her drink and listened to the record, over and over. . . .

More than the greatest love the world has ever known . . .
This is the love I'll give to you, all alone . . .

Then she got up to dance, and she danced very close. She wore spicy cologne behind her ears, nothing under her sweater. . . .

Later at dinner, off the Via Veneto, ten film people sat around her at a big table, all eyes on her, and she was charming.

Mario, the waiter, handed her a long-stemmed rose inside the menu. She took the rose but handed back the menu, whispering in Mario's ear, "*You* will fix something special for me tonight?"

"Sì, Sì," said Mario, very excitedly, and seconds later he came out of the kitchen with a four-foot-high phallic-shaped goblet filled with red wine and placed it in front of her.

She winked.

Mario perspired.

Then the musicians strolled over and played the *Mondo Cane* theme, and she listened, very content. But then, suddenly, she noticed that a tall, sophisticated brunette had captured the attention at the far end of the table. Romy could not hear the brunette's conversation, but she seemed unsettled. She quickly took out her compact, looked at her image, patted her hair. Then she got up from the table, returning five minutes later with her hair freshly combed. The woman was still holding forth, and Romy remained standing, and said, "It is hot! We go."

"But, Romy," the publicity man said, "we haven't had dessert yet!"

"It is hot!" she insisted and, turning, was followed by the press agent and his wife, by an assistant director and *his* wife, and by one of the studio photographers.

"Oh, let her go, for chrissake," said one of the men who remained at the table. "Let's have dessert."

Romy Schneider heard him, swung around. Her eyes were very cold, and her small German jaw was rigid.

"You!" she spat out, glaring at him. "You are . . . you are . . . a *FINK!*"

Then, leaving behind her gold cigarette lighter and the rose, Romy Schneider rushed from the restaurant, crossed the Via Veneto, and ran toward her hotel.

Settling for Sin,

with Style

"Willy and I started living together in Tanganyika," she said.

"No," Willy corrected, "Saint-Tropez."

"Oh, yes," she said, after a pause, wondering how she could have forgotten. "Saint-Tropez."

Elsa Martinelli, the movie actress, was sitting next to her lover, Willy Rizzo, the photographer, on a white damask sofa in an elegant hotel overlooking Central Park. It was like so many other hotels that they had chosen since their love began in the spring of 1960; it was a big, expensive, no-questions-asked hotel, and its room clerks were among the most sophisticated men in the world.

Elsa and Willy would have much preferred being married, but, since Elsa had previously been married in the Catholic Church, and since there is no divorce in Italy, it was impossible. And soon, whenever they began going out together to restaurants or cinemas around the Via Veneto, those dreaded Italian cameramen, the *papparazzi,* would lunge forward and, with persistent, sudden flashes, begin to expose the Martinelli-Rizzo romance in the press, satisfying Rome's appetite for scandal. So, one morning in September, 1960, Elsa and Willy hopped into his car and drove seven hundred miles up the coast, not stopping until they had reached the more tolerant land of the French.

Now, more than three years later, they had stopped briefly in New York en route to Hollywood, and I had been invited for breakfast to discuss openly (and for publication) what it is like these days for those who live an illegal love.

It had been 11:30 A.M. when I arrived at the hotel. The elevator man who took me to the eighth floor, and saw me walk directly toward Suite 806, paused briefly before swinging his door to a close, perhaps hoping to catch a glimpse of Elsa.

Willy answered the door. He was a smiling, lively little man with a cigarette hanging from the side of his mouth. He was perhaps an inch shorter than Elsa, who is five-seven. He had a ruddy complexion, red hair, and freckles, and did not look like an Italian born in Naples. He was wearing a pale blue shirt, open at the neck, trim tan trousers and dainty, soft-leathered shoes.

"Ah, yes," he said, bowing slightly, "you have come to write about The Big Love!" He laughed, and then shook his right hand limply in that Italian gesture signifying turbulence, raised his big brown eyes to the ceiling, and whistled soundlessly. Then he led the way into the living room, where Elsa was seated on the sofa with her bare feet tucked under her.

She was wearing one of Willy's shirts over her Capri pants; her light brown hair, still damp from the shower, was covered by a white towel twisted into a turban. On the marble coffee table in front of her were strewn telegrams and telephone messages, and to the left was a bouquet of flowers from one of Elsa's never-say-die admirers. After a minimum of formality, we got right to the subject.

"Ever since Saint-Tropez," she said, "Willy and I have been together."

"We decided after our first night, never to separate," Willy said.

"He decided," Elsa insisted, smiling.

"The *first* night?" he asked, amazed.

"All right, the second," she said, running her hand through his curly red hair and pecking him on the cheek.

"And because of this life," I said, "people say you are living in sin. Do you agree?"

"I do not," Elsa said, firmly. "But," she added, shrugging, "I do not really care what people say. I care only that Italian law prohibits me from divorcing my husband so I can marry Willy. So I am living with Willy. And we're not married. And I don't care. And everybody knows it."

"But," I asked, "hasn't your love been more or less confined to a hotel room?"

"Two hotel rooms!" Willy quickly interjected. "If we have only *one* room, we could be right away arrested for adultery. Here, in this hotel, we have two room. Elsa sleeps in that room over there," he said, pointing to the half-open door into Suite 807 that revealed a large, unmade bed, "and I sleep here, on this sofa." He smiled, patting the cushions on the sofa. "Even if we are staying in the middle of the Sahara," he went on, "and someone writes to the Italian government and can prove we sleep together in just one room, we can be arrested. But if we have a suite—two room—they cannot arrest us. The law is very nice, *non?"*

Elsa laughed. Her English is much better than his, but she seemed satisfied, even proud, of the way he was slowly choosing his words in English to describe the details, and her interruptions now were brief.

"Suppose," I asked, "you cannot get two hotel rooms adjoining?"

"Yes, in Tokyo," she reminded him, "the hotel was crowded, and we did not have two rooms together. You were on the fourth floor, and I was on the second."

"But I come down," he reminded her.

"If you get caught in bed together, what happens?" I asked.

"Well," Willy said, wincing, "anywhere in the world, if you are caught in bed with a woman not your wife, you could go right away to jail."

"True," Elsa nodded.

"*Except* in a place like France," Willy said. "In France, they do not do anything. In one room, in France, can be one man, one woman; can be two man, two woman; can be three woman, one dog. Can be two elephant. In France, it's the only country in the world. I love Paris. A real republic!

"I think France is the only country where you go to a hotel with a woman not your wife, and they care only that you have passport," Willy said. "You can give the hotel clerk two passport; you can give him three passport, four. It's nothing. In Paris, passport are for the police. Not for love."

"Strange, *non?*" Elsa asked, amused, slowly stroking his neck.

"What about hotels in New York, London, Hollywood?" I asked.

"Well," Willy continued, knowledgeably, "as I say, you must always go to a big hotel. A hotel where they have a suite. If they are full, then go to another big hotel. Just never go to a small hotel. Even in Italy, if you go to a big hotel, and get two rooms, no problem. They do not come into your room without first knocking. When they knock—*knock, knock*—you go to the sofa in the other room. You sit down."

Willy sat up primly on the sofa, arms folded, eyes toward Heaven, a look of mock innocence on his face. "Everywhere in the world, I think, they must knock first—even in America, it is the law, *non?*"

I said I did not know, but would check with the hotel manager on my way out.

"No, no!" Willy said. "Do not check with *this* hotel! Ask another hotel."

Then, after I smiled, he did too, realizing I was not serious.

"But," he went on, "I am ninety percent sure that you have no right to sleep in a hotel room with a woman anywhere in the world if she is not your wife."

"Of course," Elsa cut in, "in America, everybody do."

"Yes," Willy said, patiently, "but in America it is so easy to get a divorce."

"In America," she said, almost bitterly, "women can have their way."

"Women in America," Willy said, "are overprotected. When men come first to America, many years ago, men were so numerous—and women were so few—that the men could not touch the woman. You touch one, you go to jail."

"Yes," Elsa agreed, "they *keel* you."

"*La valeur est du à la rareté,*" he said.

"The value of something comes from its rarity," she translated.

Then she said, "In America many years ago they had one thousand men for every one woman."

"Fan*TA*Stic!" Willy said.

"The families come over much later to America," she said.

"It is very dangerous in America then," Willy said. "You have Indian."

"But in Italy," Elsa said, "the woman never have their way. In Italy, if my husband goes with another woman, it is legal; but for a woman to go with another man, it is illegal."

"No, no," Willy cut in, "it is not legal or illegal; it is that the tribunal in Italy closes its eyes for the man, but not for the woman. That is the way of Latin people. The more you go to the South, the more the woman is down."

"How come?" I asked.

"Because the more you go to the South, the closer you are to Islam," he said in a casual, perfectly logical way. "And in Islam, the woman is nothing. In Milan, it is a little different; it is more equal. In Palermo, the man is more important than the woman. In Islam, the woman is nothing. In Islam, if you are rich, you have ten wives, fifteen wives!"

"Oh," moaned Elsa.

"In Islam, if you are poor," he said, "you just have two or three wives. That is not so good."

The phone rang. Elsa unfurled from the sofa and moved across the thick rug to the other side of the room and, from the way her voice dropped to an almost whisper, it seemed probable that one of her admirers, possibly the one who had sent the flowers, was on the other end.

Willy, however, did not seem interested in who was calling; he propped his nicely-shod feet up on the coffee table, sank more deeply into the sofa, inhaled on his cigarette and proceeded to take pot shots at the Roman Catholic Church and a few dozen other religions.

"Ah, religion!" he scoffed. "It is all nonsense! Some religion, like Moslem, is against drinking. But in other religion, the priest *make* liquor! The priest in the monasteries make *Grand Marnier, Benedictine, Cointreau,* and they make it for money, for business!"

He paused for a moment. Elsa's soft voice could be faintly heard. Willy went on, "In some countries, the religion say, 'If you do *this,* you go to hell!' But other religion, in other coun-

tries, say, 'If you do *that*, you go to hell!' If you go to hell or
to heaven must depend on where you die, *non?*" he reasoned,
with a wide grin and shrug of his shoulders. "If you die in Al-
geria, and you drink, it is Moslem land and so you go to hell.
But if you die in Stockholm, you go to heaven, *non?*"

He went on like this while Elsa continued her conversation.
Finally, after about three minutes, I perceived just a trace of
curiosity (or irritation) on Willy's part. His thoughts became
less logical. His English got worse. He did not look at Elsa,
who was leaning into a chair, hand on hip, her other long leg
stretched out behind her.

I presumed this happened often—men telephoning Elsa,
men who did not know, or did not care, that Willy was her
lover. When Elsa and Willy went dancing, men cut in eagerly
and endlessly. I had also heard, from a friend at Paramount,
that Howard Hawkes has long had an eye on Elsa, her lean
lines, her delicate bones being the looks that Hawkes sup-
posedly finds irresistible. Of course, Willy's love with Elsa,
secured by neither a contract, children, nor joint bank account, did not entitle him to a husband's fit of jealousy or a
husband's inalienable right to snatch the phone away. Lovers'
telephones are delicate instruments.

Finally, Elsa hung up. She went into the bedroom to get a
fresh pack of cigarettes, and then, when she came back, she
pecked Willy on the cheek and sat down next to him.

"How did you two first meet?" I quickly asked, fearing that
the interruption might have cooled them toward further dis-
cussion of their life.

"Well," Willy said, "I first see Elsa in October, 1958, in New
York. I was sent here by *Paris Match* to photograph the Queen
Elizabeth visit, but then I get sick in New York with Asiatic
flu, and I stay ten days in sleep. . . ."

"In bed, not sleep," Elsa corrected, softly.

"In bed," he repeated. "Anyway, the first day I get up, I go to El Morocco and John Perona introduce me to Elsa. I thing she is a snob. We dance—that's all. Not too much feeling then, *non?*"

"None at all," she answered, her head back against the sofa.

"So," he went on, "in May, 1960, Elsa come to Paris to make a French film, and *Vogue* ask me to photograph a segment of Elsa. I telephone Elsa and say, 'I'm Rizzo, you remember I dance with you?' "

"I did not remember," Elsa recalled, holding up her nose in her own imitation of snobbery.

"But we get along very nice together that day in my studio," Willy said. Elsa smiled, remembering. She now seemed cheerful again.

"After," Willy said, "I ask Elsa, 'What you are doing tomorrow for dinner?' This is the first words I learn in English. She say, 'I have dinner, but maybe I arrange.' "

"We stayed out until two o'clock in the morning," Elsa recalled, her eyebrows raised almost in girlish delight.

"We had dinner at La Louisiana, on St.-Germain-des-Près, a little bistro," Willy said.

"Wonderful," she said.

"Very nice, very nice, *ve-ry* constructive," he said. *"Nous parlions le même langage."*

"We spoke the same language," she repeated.

After her film in Paris was completed and she was scheduled to return to Rome, they knew they did not want to be apart for long, and so Willy decided to return to Rome with her. He arranged to rent a small apartment a safe distance from where Elsa was living with her husband, Count Franco Mancinelli Scotti.

"After that," Willy said, "the big love."

"And the difficult love," Elsa said, adding, "Oh, how they love scandal in Rome!"

"Fan*TA*Stic!" Willy said. "In Rome," he said, tapping on my knee, "if you have lunch with Elsa, the next day you hear you are Elsa's new lover."

"Sometimes," Elsa said, "the newspapers will get a picture of two people, cut the picture in half, and show them sitting at different tables and say they had a fight."

"*Bad* journalism," Willy declared.

"I could not go out of the house," she said. "They were downstairs waiting."

"They even had a telephoto lens on my apartment," Willy said.

Once, she recalled, while she was at Willy's apartment sitting down to the dinner they had just cooked, there was a knock on the door. Opening it, Elsa saw glaring at her two detectives, an attorney, and her husband, the Count. They took her to court. But there really was no sordid evidence against her; she really *was* having dinner, and the case was dismissed. But it made a delicious scandal in the newspapers.

After that, Elsa said, she pressed for a separation. In August, 1960, she obtained it. She moved her daughter, her mother, and the nurse into a large apartment. Willy maintained his smaller flat. The two of them made no attempt from then on to conceal their love. After the trip to Saint-Tropez, they began living regularly in hotels—and have continued to ever since. When she is making a film, she requests that the producer hire Willy to make the publicity photographs. During the rare hours they spend apart, they keep in touch by telephone. In a sense, they are more closely bound than the most united of married couples. Marriage might even free them a bit. But there is no chance of marriage, they say; and this makes them bitter.

"Our religion, Catholic, says every man can make a mistake and God pardons," Willy said. "You kill, and you have a pardon. But you make a mistake in marriage, no pardon. Why? If we were French, or American, or English, or anything else but Italian—or Spanish—there is no problem; there the law is different. My wife, Paule, is French, and she got a divorce from me and, six months later, she is married again!"

"A human being cannot be perfect," Elsa said. "Marriage, after all, is made mostly under a sentiment that is instantaneous—*love*. You don't plan love. You just fall in love. And then, love can grow, or love can be less. The first time you fall in love, it's always on instinct. And then, if you are lucky, you discover more than love. Of course, this makes love more important. But it can also happen that this sentiment can be mistaken. And love finishes. And there is not anything else."

"So," Willy said, "because the Church controls the State in Italy, we are a scandal!"

"In Italy," Elsa said, "my maid have the same problem I have. Of course, I can go my way. And my feeling is different than my maid. Maids," she said, sighing, "they are scared. Their husband can do anything he wants. They can go to jail and cannot even afford a lawyer. It is ridiculous!"

"Well," I said, lightly, "maybe if the Communists take over Italy you will not have to worry about the Catholic law there and you and Willy may get married."

"Yes," Willy said, "but I prefer the Catholic Church to the Communists."

"Let's say you prefer not being married to being a Communist," Elsa said.

"Yes," Willy nodded, "I say that."

"Why can't you leave Italy and become a citizen of another country?"

"It is not easy," Willy said.

"You have to ask first that another country accepts you," Elsa said. "In America, for instance, this takes, I think, at least five years. It would take more than five years to get married. So, today, many of our Italian friends live just like we do. It is considered the normal thing."

"What are some of the things you most dislike about this life?"

"Well," she said, "take this hotel suite. It is a *little* embarrassing. I mean, I would rather register here as Mr. and Mrs. Willy Rizzo instead of registering under our separate names and taking two rooms.

"And," she continued, "my husband in Rome, he can still bring an adultery charge against me for the rest of my life if he can prove I live under the same roof with a man. I can go to jail. Also, if I want to bring my daughter to Paris, or someplace else, he does not permit it." (Elsa's daughter, now six years old, remains with Elsa's mother and the nurse in the apartment in Rome.)

"There is another thing," Elsa said. "To me, there comes a moment when you and the person you love want very much to have a child. Well, I am lucky I have already a child. And Willy is lucky, too, because he has two children with his former wife. So we—Willy and myself—are not now planning to have children. But if I had no child, and if I had a child by Willy, that child would take the name of my husband; or, if my husband did not want to give his name to the child, then the child would take *my* name—but never Willy's name. But if Willy and I did not have children already, I would have one with Willy. What's the difference?"

"What does your mother think of your life?"

"Well," Elsa said, "my mother, she, of course, wants me to be happy. She would like it if I were married, of course. But I think she likes to see me happy with Willy more than the way I was with my husband."

She had met the Count in the winter of 1954 at a ski resort near Torino. Elsa was then nineteen—a tall, flighty high-fashion model earning $1,000 a week and embarking on a movie career. In 1957—over the protests of the Count's mother, who did not believe in a "mixed" marriage between a nobleman and an actress—Elsa and the Count were married. A year or so later, Elsa realized the marriage had been a terrible mistake.

"My problem was that my husband never worked a day in his life," Elsa said. "And he was used to going to every dinner party in Rome. Of course, I was getting up in the morning to work, and we had a daughter, and the problem was to follow him. And I did, for two years. Sometimes we would go somewhere to stay three days—and we would stay three months."

"Fan*TA*Stic!" Willy exclaimed.

Then Willy said, lighting Elsa's cigarette, "You know, Elsa was so stup-*id,* so cra-*zee* during those years; after she make her first American picture with Kirk Douglas [*Indian Fighter,* 1957] she have many, many propositions to do other films, but she say, 'No.' "

"I want to go to the beach," Elsa explained.

"Yes," he agreed, "when they offer her a film, she say, 'No, I am sorr-*ee,* I go to Capri—I have a friend with a boat!' " Then he thought for a moment, looked at her and said, "Oh, if you had the same mentality six years ago that you have now, you could be Elizabeth Taylor today."

"Maybe Elizabeth Taylor is not a very good example," I quickly cut in.

"One million dollars a picture is a good example," Willy insisted.

Then he said, almost philosophically, "You know, I think it is very Italian to live from day to day, as Elsa did. Now I work most of the time with American model and they are perfect, they are always ready for work at nine o'clock. But when I am working with Italian model, and have an appointment for nine o'clock, she comes in at ten-thirty and says, 'Oh, I am so sorry, darling, my boy friend is ill, and . . .' The Italian model," he went on, "she is nice; she is beautiful; she is everything. But, for work, she is terrible!"

"I do not regret one single day of my life!" Elsa snapped. "I think you learn much more from bad experiences than good ones."

"Yes," Willy nodded, "yes, but the American girl, when she decide to work, she *work*."

"What about Sophia?" Elsa said.

"Oh, yes," he agreed, nodding, "Sophia Loren and Lollobrigida, they work. True. And all the time I see Sophia and Carlo Ponti, they talk business. Movie business. All the time. The machine."

"Too much," Elsa said.

"Yes," Willy finally conceded, "there is a middle."

It was now 1 P.M. and the afternoon sun was shining brightly through the hotel windows. Elsa and Willy sat quietly for a moment, smoking and thinking; and then Elsa realized that breakfast had not yet been ordered. So she stood, picked up the phone, and requested that menus be brought up.

Willy watched her; she has changed a great deal from her early modeling days in 1955, he said. Now she is the most beautiful woman he has ever seen, and is dedicated to the task of becoming a fine actress.

"Elsa now understand the work, the real work," Willy said. "She understand the work and the good friend. The little dinner for three or four. Elsa do not know this before. Now she do. Very nice. She like very much now."

"But how long can this life go on?" I asked, after she had returned to the sofa.

"The rest of our life," Elsa said.

"Forever," Willy said.

"I'm sure it shall be," she said.

"I hope so," he said.

ABANDONING

For many years they have lived happily
in New York and were convinced,
along with E. B. White,
that the city was a kind of marvelous,
gigantic man-made womb;
it bestowed the gift of privacy,
the jewel of loneliness,
the vibrations of great times—and
it also seemed insulated against shock.
   Then, rather suddenly, they no longer
felt safe in New York. The Berlin crisis
had worsened, and many New Yorkers—
shaken by the shelter syndrome,
harassed by "Ban the Bomb" pacifists,
suspicious of the morning's milk delivery—
believed that their city was now
the world's No. 1 bomb target.

NEW YORK

IV

So, in the fall of 1961, twenty-five New Yorkers
who had become quite friendly
in recent years met at a suburban home
in Smithtown, Long Island, and decided
they would abandon the city together;
and one morning two weeks later,
after packing their furniture, their ten children,
their three cats and Afghan hound
into a dozen vehicles, they rolled in a caravan
across the country into a small northern
California city called Chico, which,
according to their interpretation
of Atomic Energy Commission data,
was fallout free.
     And now, three years later,
they are still there . . .
               still alive.

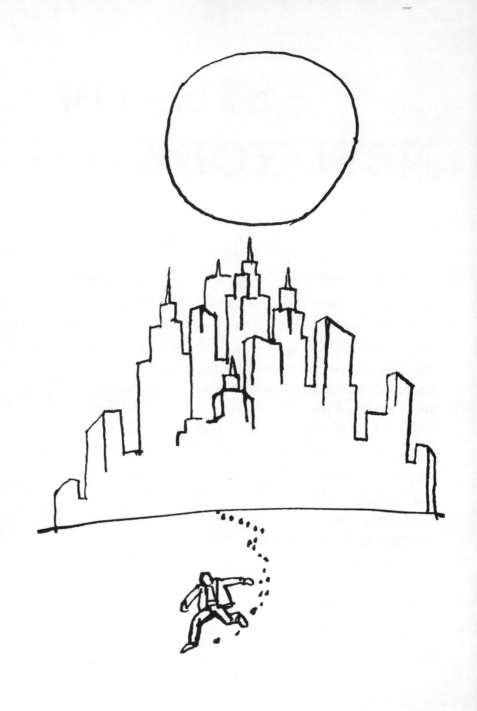

...The City They Left Behind

The branches are still bare in Washington Square Park, but Greenwich Village folk singers are out in force—and beatniks are in bloom. They all sit or slumber along the edge of the park's pool and sing sad ballads together, or listen to the competitive strumming of the guitar players, or just wander through the crowds.

"Marsha," says a blonde girl in a dark sweater, tight pants, and sneakers, "see that guy?"

"Yes," says Marsha.

"Think he's good-looking?"

"*Yes-s-s,*" says Marsha.

"He goes to Bellevue each week for shots."

"He's a gem," says Marsha, full of understanding.

Ten yards from them a quartet sings "Down by the River Side," and twenty yards away larger crowds gather to watch

a lasso being twirled by a Manhattan cowboy who calls himself Texas Weinstein, but who is known to the NYU students
as "Moshe Mix." Behind him a slinky girl sits reading Proust,
her expression hidden behind sunglasses. Next to her is a
monkey on a chain who seems interested in the poetry that
William Brown, a Negro poet, is delivering to his followers
on the other side of the pool.

> ". . . *he choked-up* tight . . .
> *in his white-on-*white," says the poet,
> "*and he wore a cocoa-brown* . . . that was down *a candy-
> striped tie* . . .
> *and he looked real* fly . . .
> *and he had on a gold-dust* crown . . .
> *and it was the fourteenth* frame *of a nine-ball* game . . .
> *and as Bud stood watching the play, with a casual shrug, he
> looked up and* dug . . .
> *a strange cat coming his way* . . ."

The young people at his knee seem visibly moved by his
lines and, when he finishes, they put money in his hand.

"Splendid," says the poet, "my money has turned *green* . . .
on the New York *scene*. . . ."

Then a very intense girl in horn-rimmed glasses places a
half-eaten Popsicle into his hand.

"Splendid," he exclaims, and then vanishes into the crowds
that are now clustered in the sun, singing out such questions as,

> *"Oh, where have all those
> Young girls gone?
> To husbands every one
> Oh, when will they ever
> Learn?
> Oh, when will they* . . ."

It is a beautiful, peaceful day in New York, and they sing on and on . . . undisturbed by the children on tricycles scooting under their guitars . . . undisturbed by the boys who hurl pink high-bouncers past them . . . undisturbed by the Bomb.

SUMMER

IN

NEW YORK

Times Square is snapping to the ragtime rhythm of shoe-shine boys; Central Park is billowing with balloons, and, on the edge of the Hudson River, a tall, chesty man stands in the sun, all alone, playing a saxophone. It is a summer day with melody and mood for those who have not abandoned the city—a day in which people do most of the same things that they would have done had they gone elsewhere to escape the heat. They sunbathe on rooftops, picnic in parks, cycle through streets, stroll along sidewalks, swim in the pools of West Side motels, or take a luxury cruise for a penny a mile.

For more than three hundred years, or ever since Staten Island was settled in 1661, the ferryboat has been a kind of hound's hare for seagulls, a splashing adventure for small boys, and an ideal spot for romantics who have no particular desire to reach the other side. It provides air-conditioning on sweltering evenings, and gives esthetes a chance to back off and admire the view of lower Manhattan—the tall, thin buildings bunched together like celery and shooting skyward; the whole glittering island seemingly floating in the river and resembling, in Truman Capote's words, a "diamond iceberg." This scene is accompanied by a symphony of sea sounds—the clanging buoy bells, the low groans of tugs, and the high-pitched squeals of seagulls that follow in flight and then swoop down at the churned-up seafood in the foamy wake of the ferry. When the ferry completes the five-mile journey to Staten Island, and bumps into the U-shaped slip, these salty scavengers perch on the pilings and wait impatiently for the ferryboat to reload, the captain to give two hoots to the horn, and for the engines to begin to bubble back toward Manhattan and stir up more food for seagulls in Upper Bay.

A few blocks away from the ferry pier, on a plot of sidewalk dirt not much larger than a pizza pie, a Puerto Rican porter named Juan Negron is casually growing stalks of corn four feet high; nobody told him that corn will not grow along the sidewalks of New York. Further uptown, near the Americana Hotel on Fifty-second Street, a blind man in a straw hat is singing "If I Didn't Care"—and people toss coins at his feet. And ten blocks north, Central Park's benches are still elbow to elbow with people, most of whom sit cross-legged, exchanging conversations that, to passing eavesdroppers, are but a stream-of-conscious blend: ". . . and I want to tell ya, Lyndon Johnson is . . . three nice buttons, it's a two-piece . . . you don't have to do anything, Harry, don't worry . . . *ven aca, ven aca, Carlito!* . . . And I said, look, Mary . . . yeah, there's only one way to do it, your way! . . . World War II they had eleven million soldiers . . . and I said . . . 'the score is 4–3 Boston, last of the ninth [transistor radio], Mantle at third, Maris at first, Pepitone the hitter' . . . I didn't know what to wear. . . . Sarah, get over here, baby. . . . 'It's a 4–4 ball game, that's all for Earl Wilson.' . . ."

Throughout the park, throughout the day, the movement continues: perambulators, wheel chairs; parents chasing children, people clutching transistors, Popsicles, baseball bats;

people in Bermuda shorts, T-shirts, shantung suits; all of them enjoying a warm Sunday in New York, none of them contemplating a nuclear burial. And, in Central Park, the lion sleeps. . . .

WINTER

IN

NEW YORK

In winter New York is heavily seasoned with street salt, and the wind blows snow up coat sleeves, down boots, and into the eyes of pedestrians—blurring their view of nature's triumph. It is a triumph unapplauded by New Yorkers who have to shovel, or commute, or work outdoors; and it is a dark, unprofitable day for restaurateurs and shoeshine boys, for outdoor poets and sidewalk singers. But for those who are romantic about the seasons, and are not intimidated by change, it is a magnificent day in New York.

There are skiers in Van Cortlandt Park, skaters in Rockefeller Center, and a swinging pushboy in the Garment Center who moves his hips behind the rack he pushes and the radio that sings out: *"I'm sure you know I loves you, baby, with all my hah-heart. . . ."* Watching the snow from the window of her Seventh Avenue cosmetics shop, Mrs. Ethel Lussier, a Minnesota native, becomes nostalgic. "I love it," she says. "I love the feel of snow crunching under your feet. When it snows in Minnesota you feel you want to skip work and take off for the next big hill with a toboggan. . . . Sure, I had to wait a little longer this morning in the subway, and walked a little more cautiously. But that's all right. . . ."

It is quieter, softer, less crowded in New York. There are

fewer cars in town. It is easy to get a ticket to a hit show. Kinney's parking lots are off 60 percent. Schools are closed. And students come howling down the hills of Central Park on sleds, bumping buoyantly, scarves blowing in the breeze—they are *free,* free as only the very young can be on sunny days when the snow is everywhere, and schools are closed. So New York becomes their private playground, and they build fortresses along Amsterdam Avenue, slide through Sutton Place, dance atop parked cars in snowdrifts.

Throughout the day the radio reports gloomy details about the "storm" and "blizzard" and "blinding snow" and "thrashing waves," but business in New York goes on. Many people complain, but they go on, too. Gristede's delivery boys bend low behind their wagons. Bus drivers squint in the swirling snow scene, and pedestrians seem prematurely gray as they trudge up and down streets with half-opened umbrellas, half-closed eyes. "Watch the lights, watch the lights, watch the lights, lady—damnit!" shouts a Sanitation driver to a woman crossing Seventy-third Street against traffic. She tightens her lip, glares. On Times Square at 2:41 P.M., a man slips and falls on his head.

"Christ," he yells. Then he gets up. He brushes himself off. He continues on.

New York is not for the timid. It is not for those who seek the security of Chico. New York is where there might occur at any moment, any second, an event that may surprise, tantalize, shock, or destroy . . . where a jet liner suddenly smashes into Brooklyn . . . where two dozen telephone girls are quickly blown up by a boiler blast on Broadway . . . where a woman is murdered one night in Queens while nearly forty people idly listen . . . where life and death largely depend on luck.

New York is often portrayed as a city of Fun People, of witty, successful sophisticates dashing to parties or stepping out of Bentleys into theatres, but this is only part of New York. New York is also a lonely city, perhaps the loneliest city in America, and each night its streets are shadowed by the solitary silhouettes of those who have nowhere to go, nobody to talk to, nothing to do.

On an average night in the south Bronx, patrolman William Giddings walks five miles, issues one parking ticket, breaks up two family fights, and tussles with two or three winos who insist upon sleeping in hallways. He does all this without thinking too deeply about it; eighteen years on the force have introduced him to so many of New York's unpredictabilities that he is rarely shocked, surprised, or disappointed either by what he sees or does.

New York is a mad, marvelous city of too many people, too many cars, of too few triumphs and endless battles. It is the toughest town in the league, full of curves—the perfect town for Overreachers—those who will take that extra step, lean too far, go too fast, get too grabby with the gods.

In this city Frank Costello succeeded without honor, Joshua Logan succeeded without happiness, and Floyd Patterson succeeded without knowing it. It is where millions of others have sought the fulfillment of their dreams, s-t-r-e-t-c-h-e-d out and reached and overreached . . . and got their fingers chopped off.

It is a tough, unsentimental town in which nobody wins for very long. Sooner or later, everybody winds up like the elevator men, men who helped lift New York to its greatest heights but now are being replaced by electronic buttons and doors that are deaf to the cry "Hold it, please." Even the Empire State Building, the symbol of New York, is threatened because now the city plans to overreach itself with two 110-story skyscrapers downtown, and all over New York sentimentalists are hoping it won't happen, but wiser men know that sooner or later it will: it is an old Greek idea.

Format by Katharine Sitterly
Set in Linotype Times Roman
Composed by American Book–Stratford Press
Printed by Murray Printing Company
Bound by American Book–Stratford Press
HARPER & ROW, PUBLISHERS, INCORPORATED